Preview Page

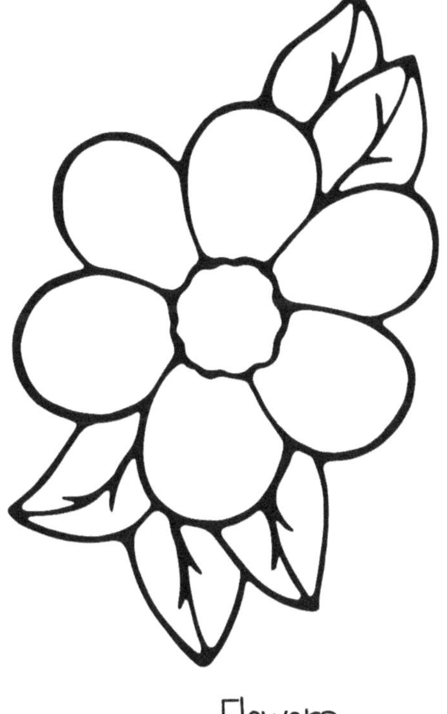

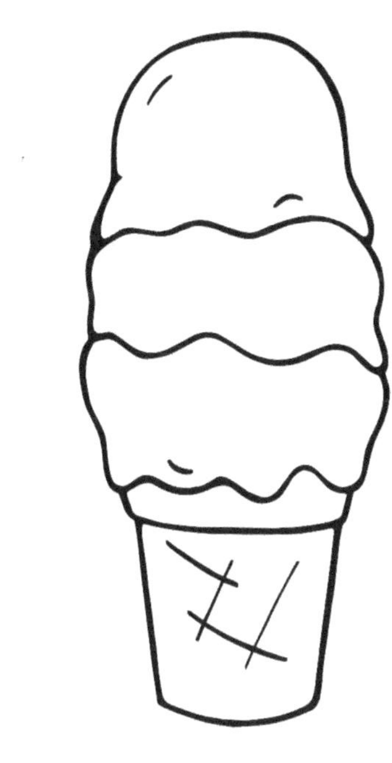

_______ Flowers

3 _______ Of Icecream

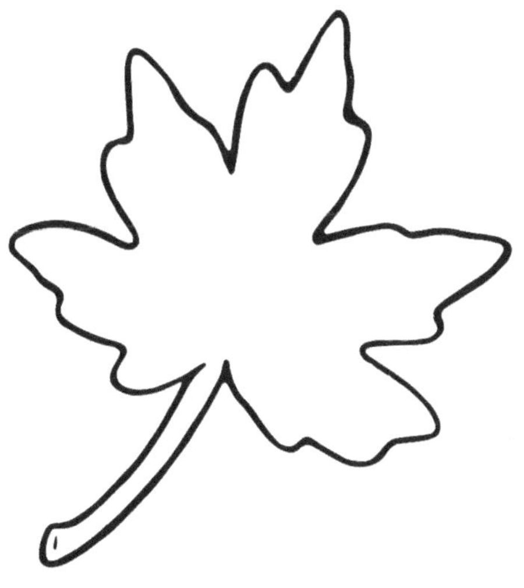

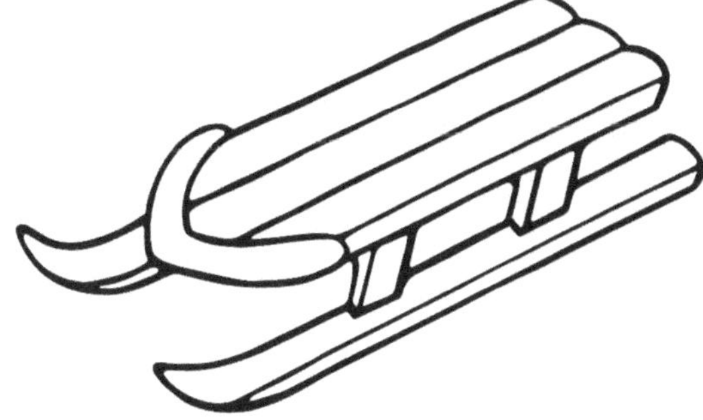

_______ Autumn Leaves

Sledding On _______

Remembering The 4-Seasons

Book 1 of 3

This Coloring Book Is Designed With Simple Familiar Black-Line Drawings
With Sentence Cuing Common Phrases For Cognitive Art Therapy - For All Ages
Recommended At Home One On One, With A Caregiver Or Family Member
And As A Resource For Therapeutic Recreation Departments.

30 Single Sided Coloring Pages, Plus
8 Keepsake Season Inspired Journal Pages

The Adult Coloring Book Craze Is Here.

Bonnie has created a great activities resource that can be used individually
on a one on one basis or in a group setting. It's simple familiar designs,
color-cuing and common phrases allow for successful completion.
Providing a positive, calm and fun experience.
I highly recommend it's use with anyone with cognitive impairment.
Every therapeutic recreation department should utilize this amazing
resource as they will immediately see the denefits.
Recommended By; Alexis Chiucarello, Director Of Therapeutic Recreation
And Dementia Program Coordinator Long Term Center.

Illustrator and Author: Bonnie S. MacLachlan

Publisher: Art.Z illustrations
Griswold, Ct
ArtZillustrations.com

Special Thanks To: Alexis Chiucarello

Made In America

Art.Z illustrations
ISBN-13: 978-09977889-0-7
ISBN-10: 0997788909

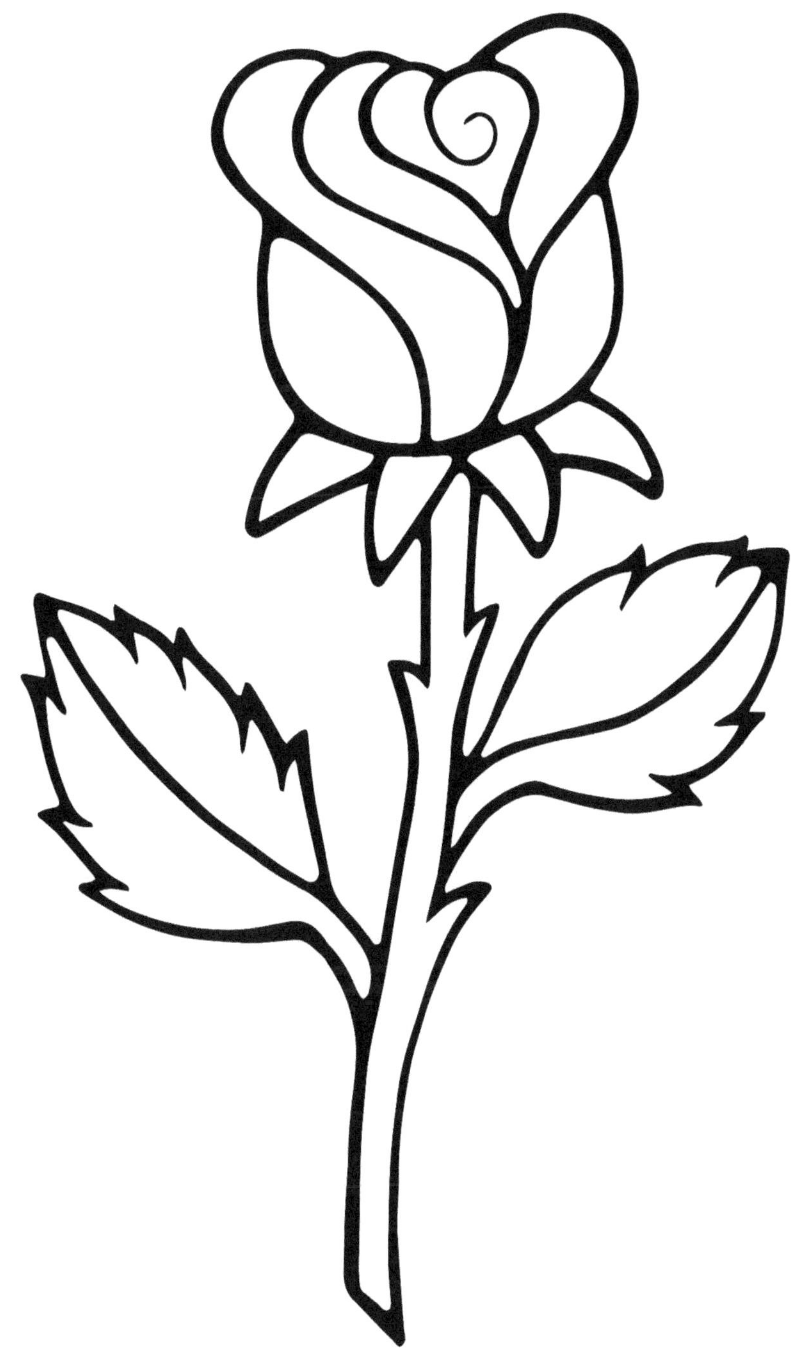

Roses Bloom In ___________

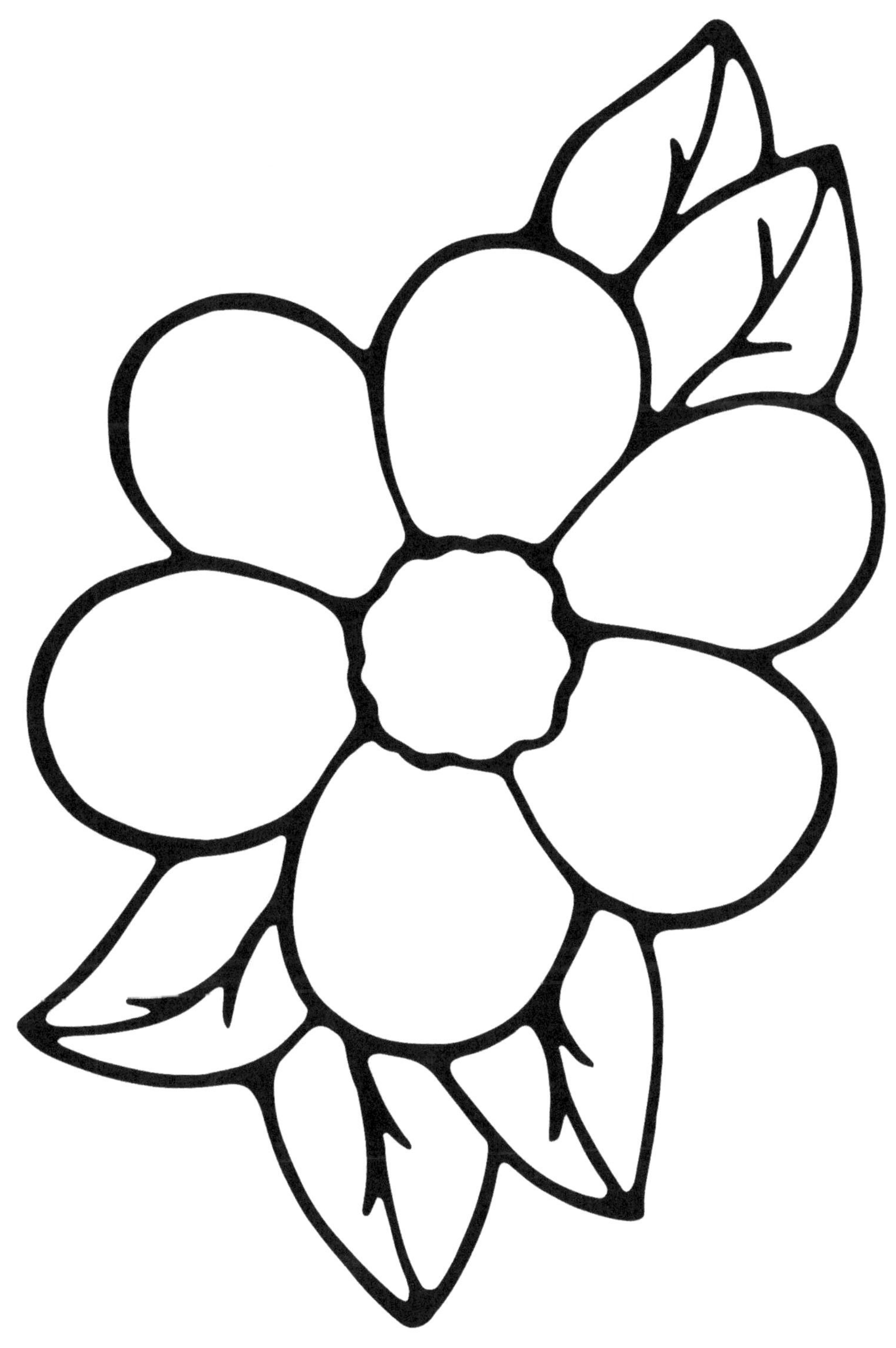

Flower ______________

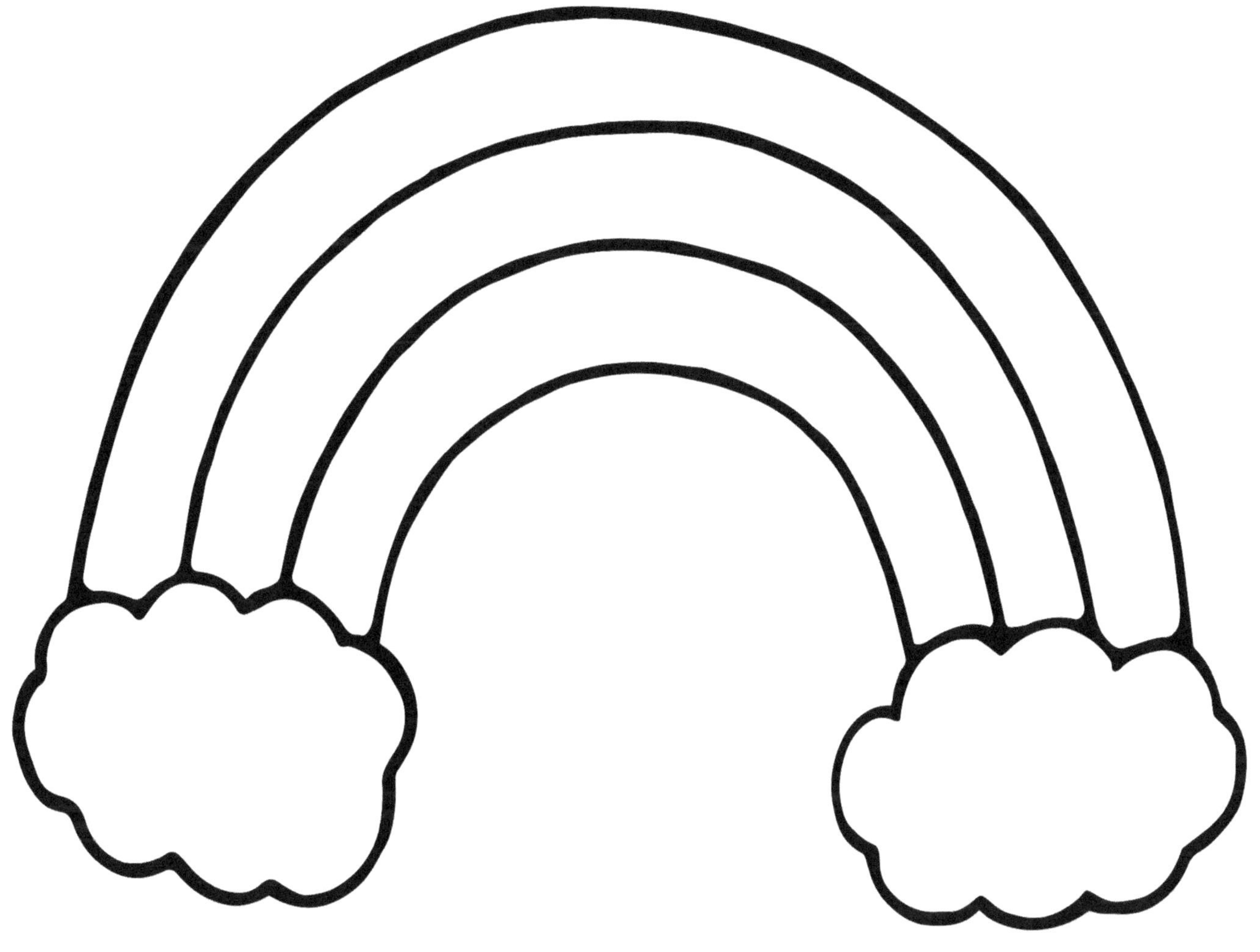

When It __________ Look For A Rainbow

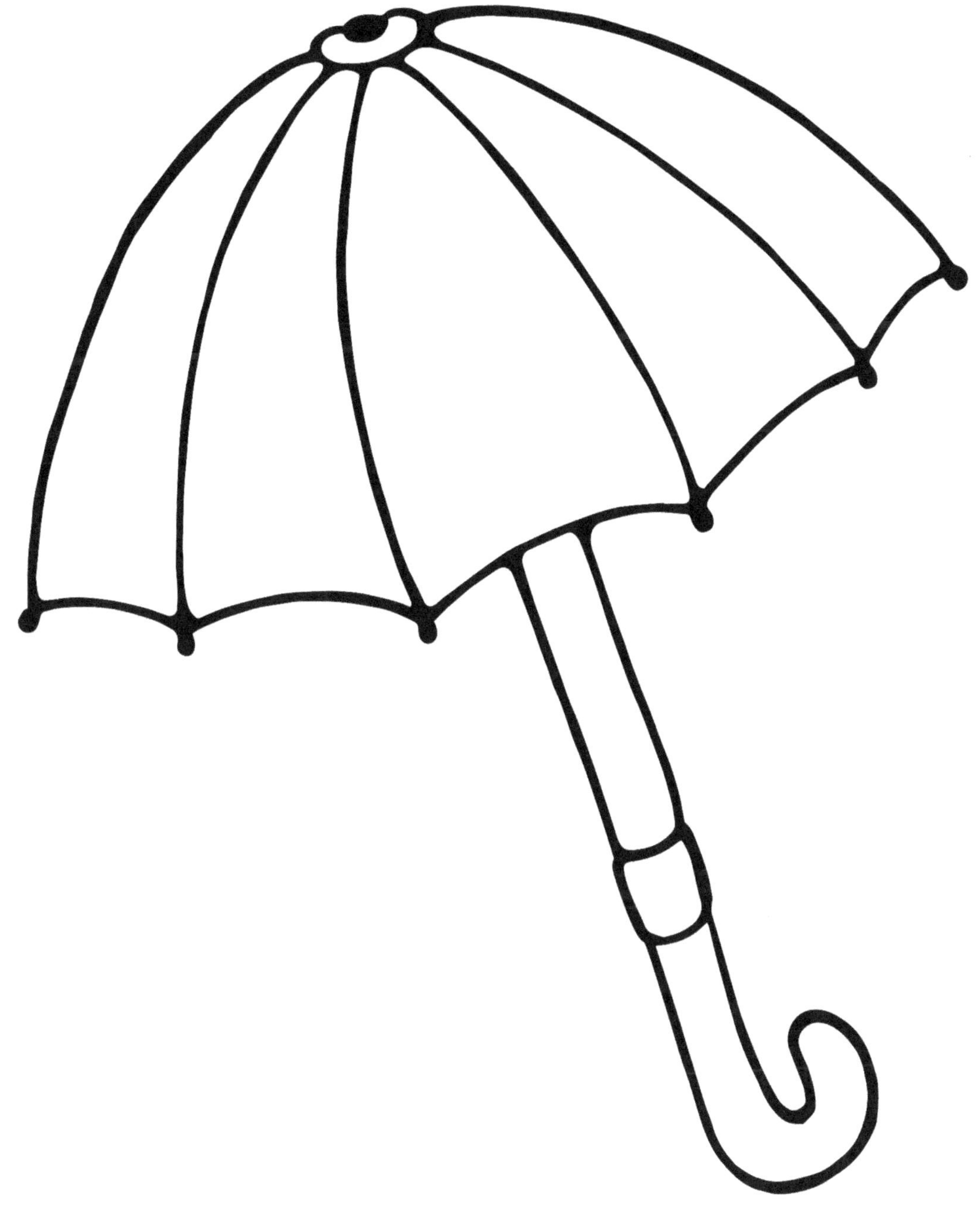

When It Rains _______ And _______, Get An Umbrella

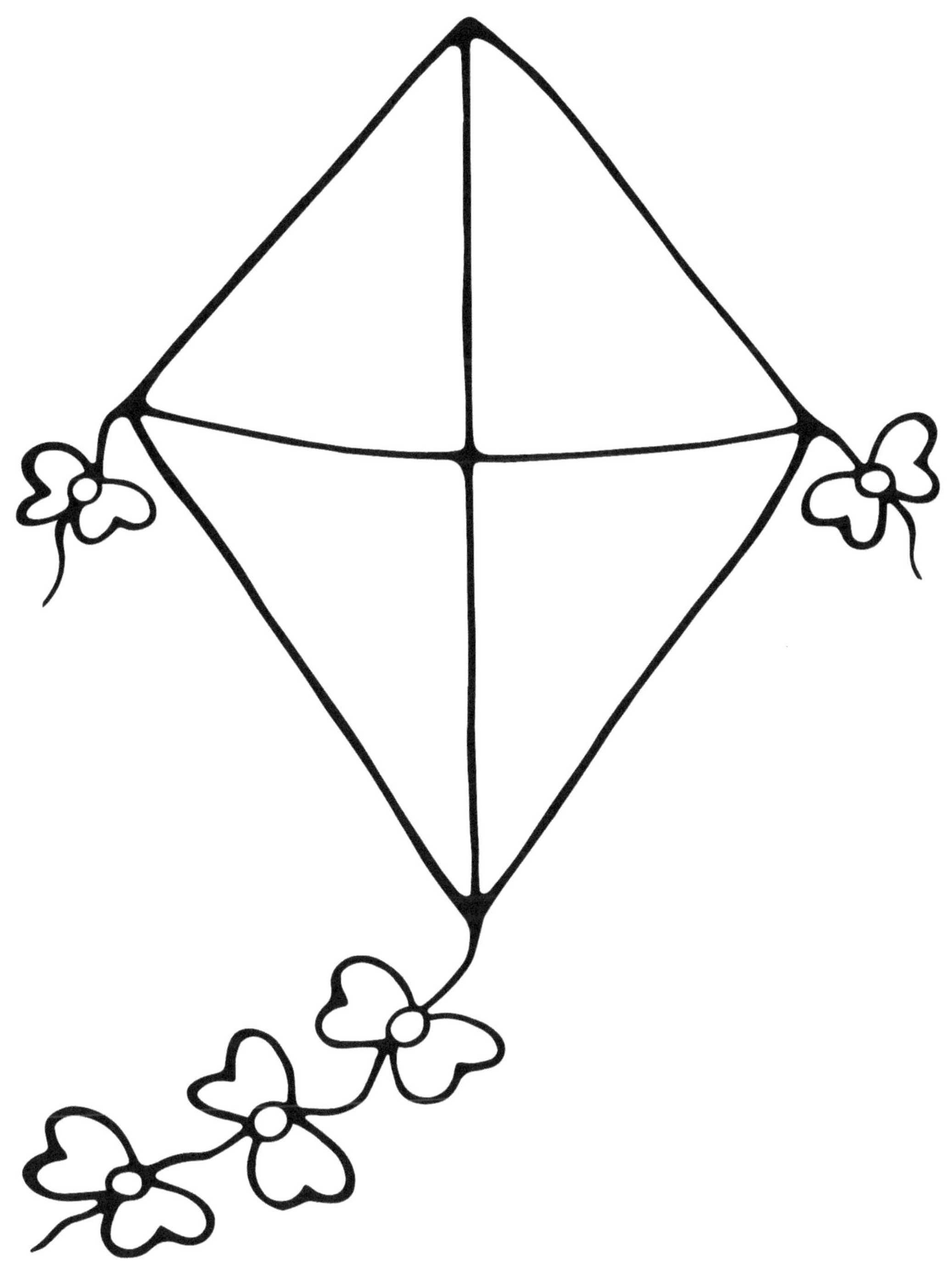

Go ______________ A Kite

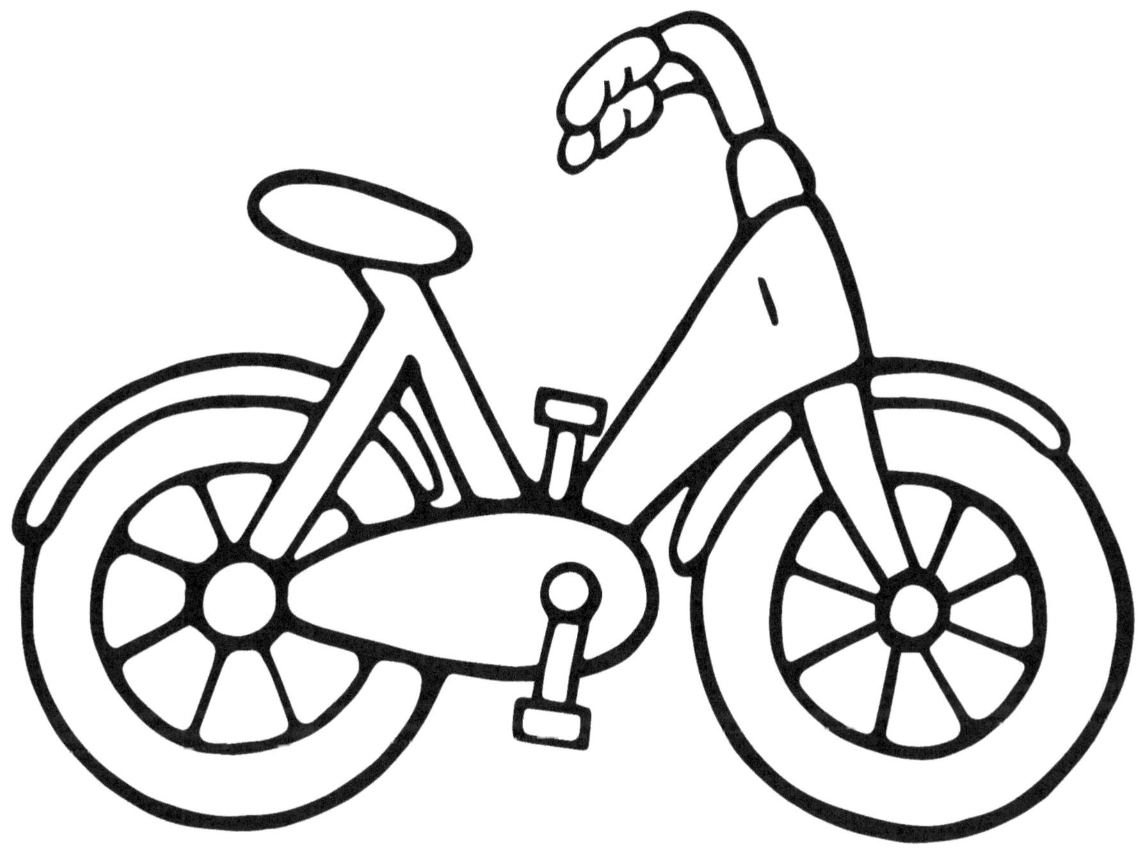

I ________ My Bike
All Over Town

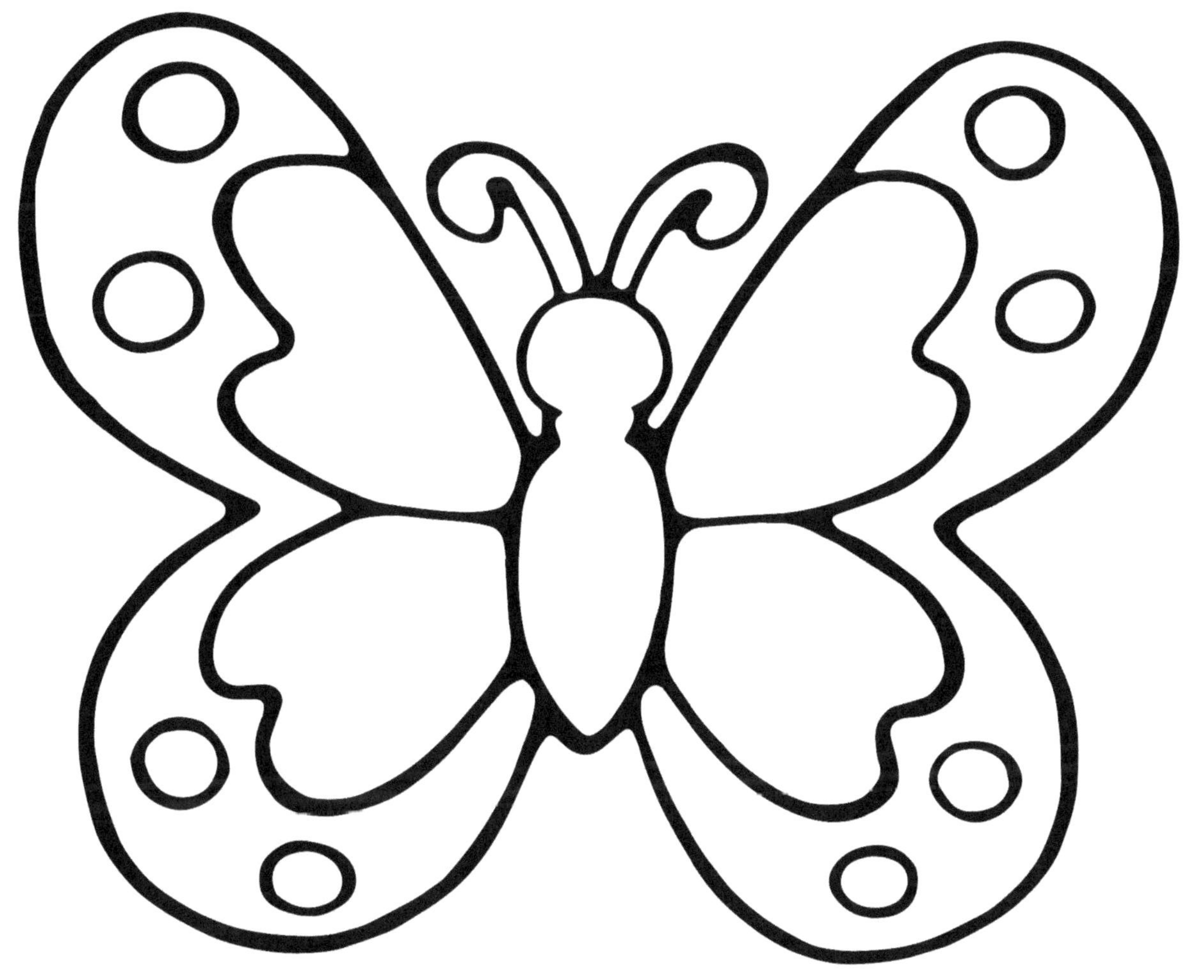

_______________ Butterflies

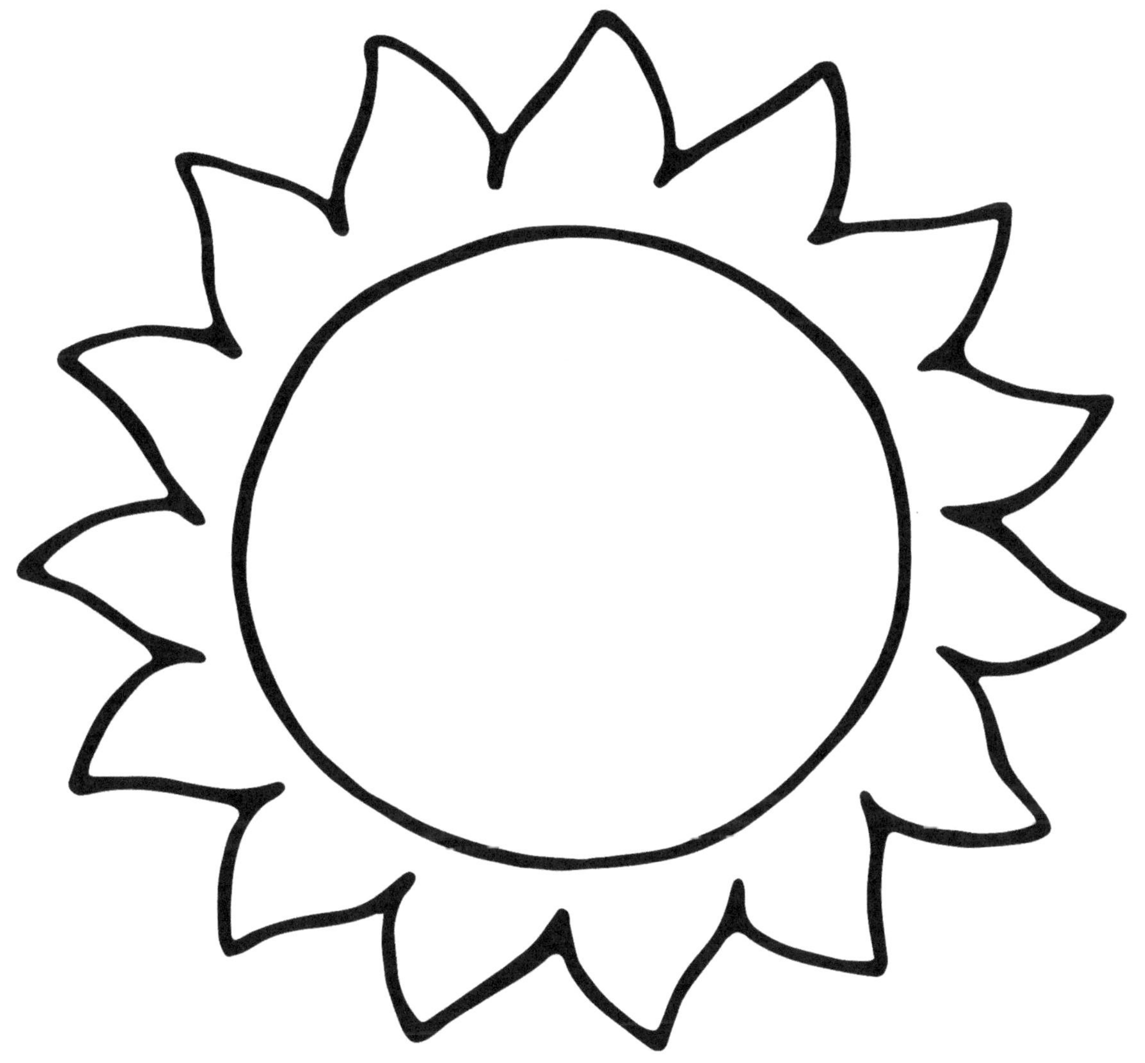

Good ____________ Sunshine

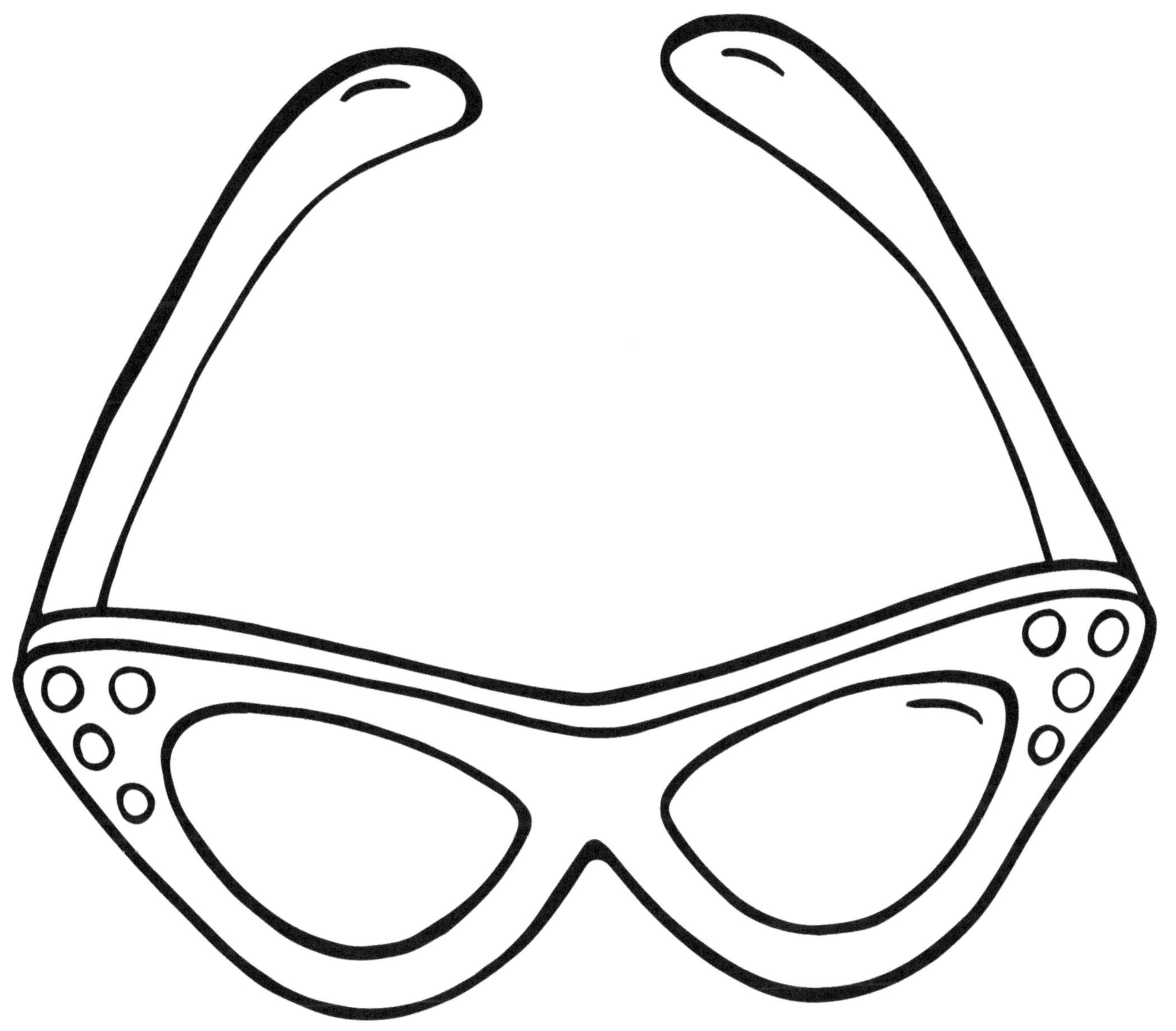

________________ Glasses

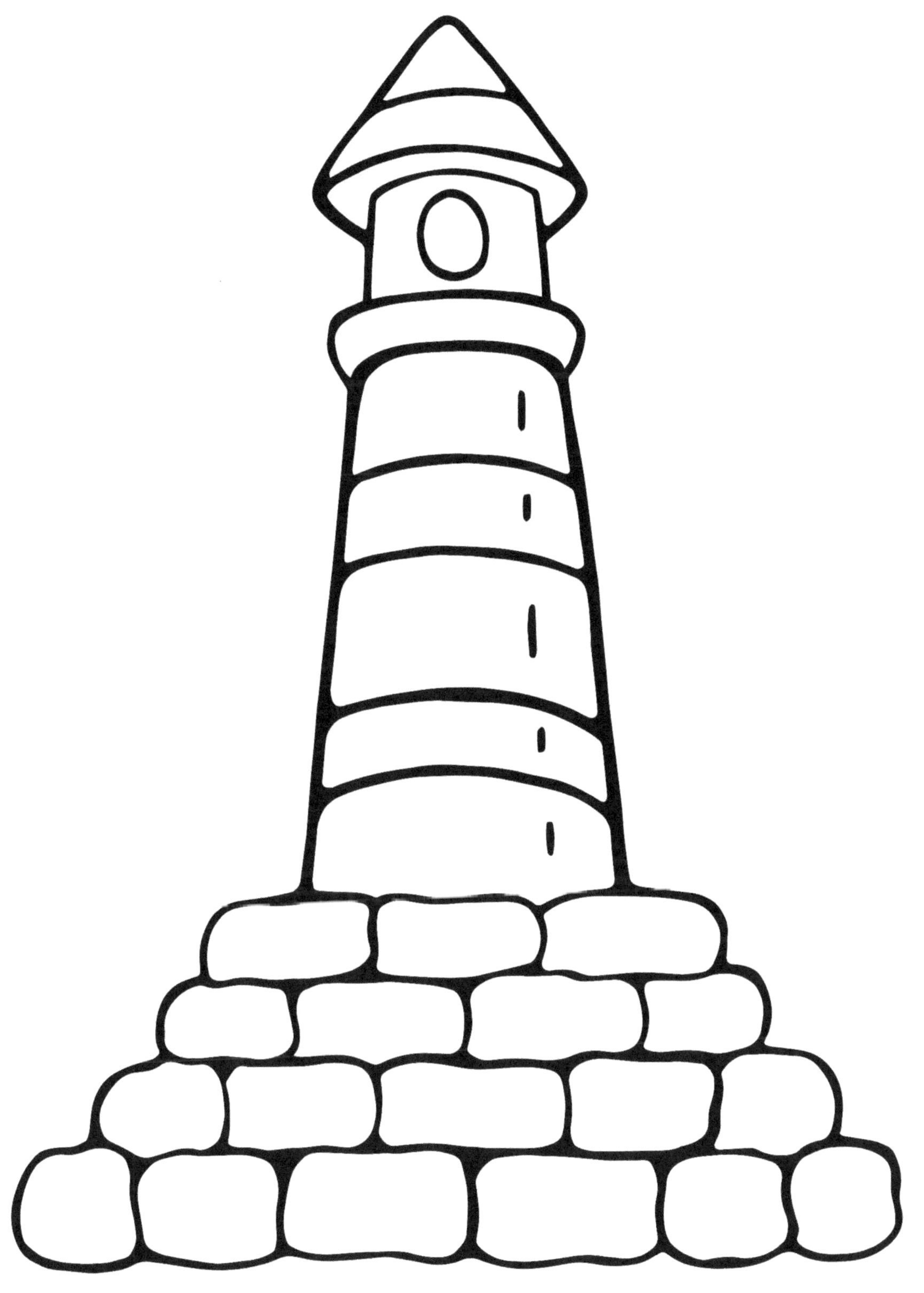

A Light House In The __________

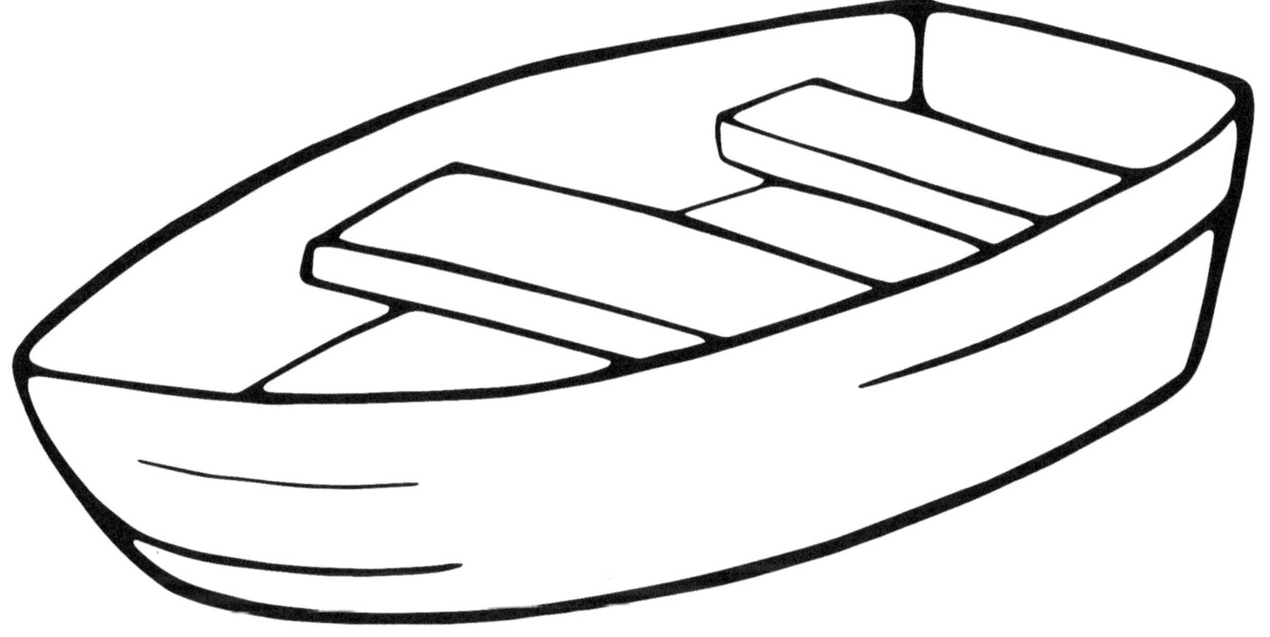

Don't ________ The Boat

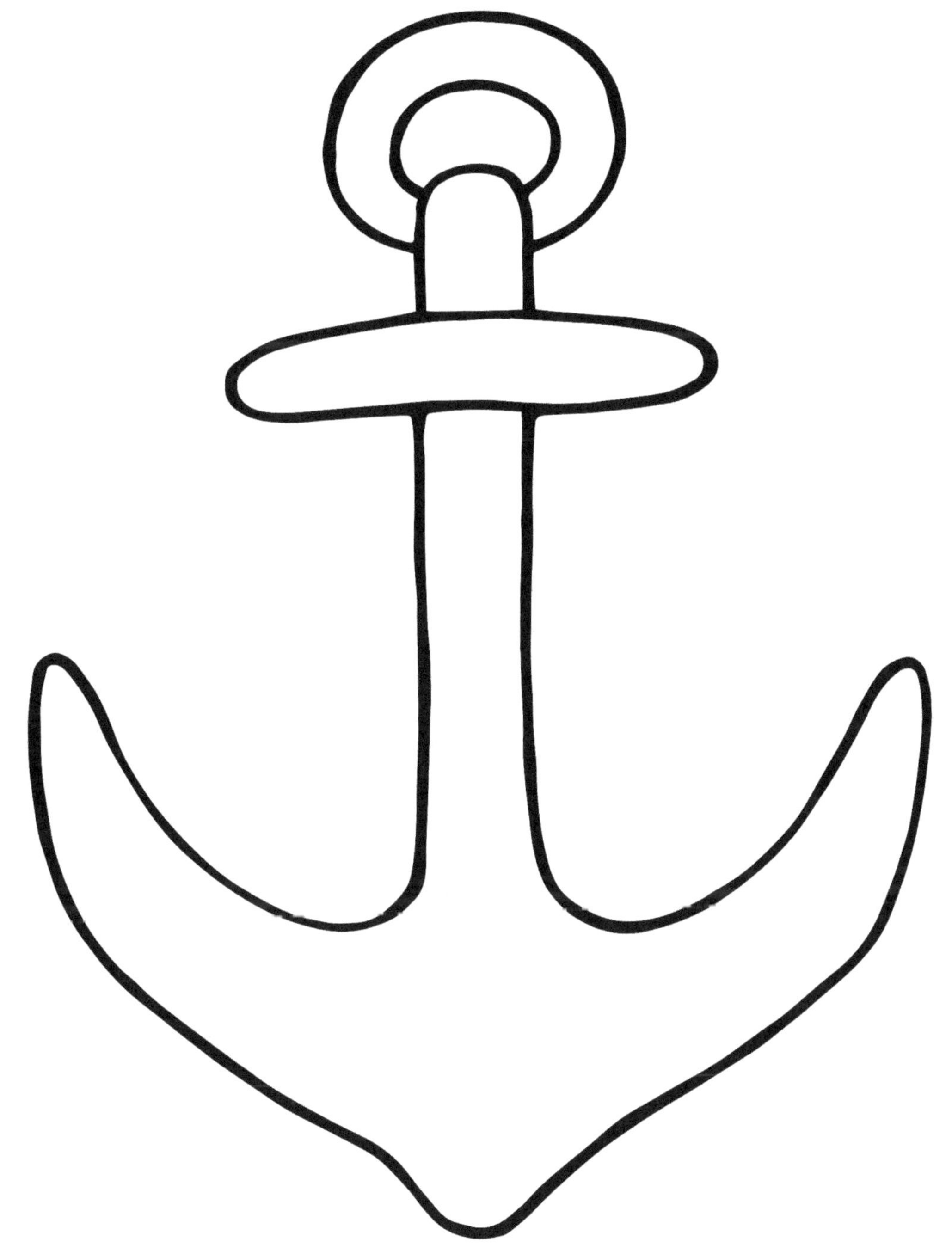

Drop The Anchor Over ______

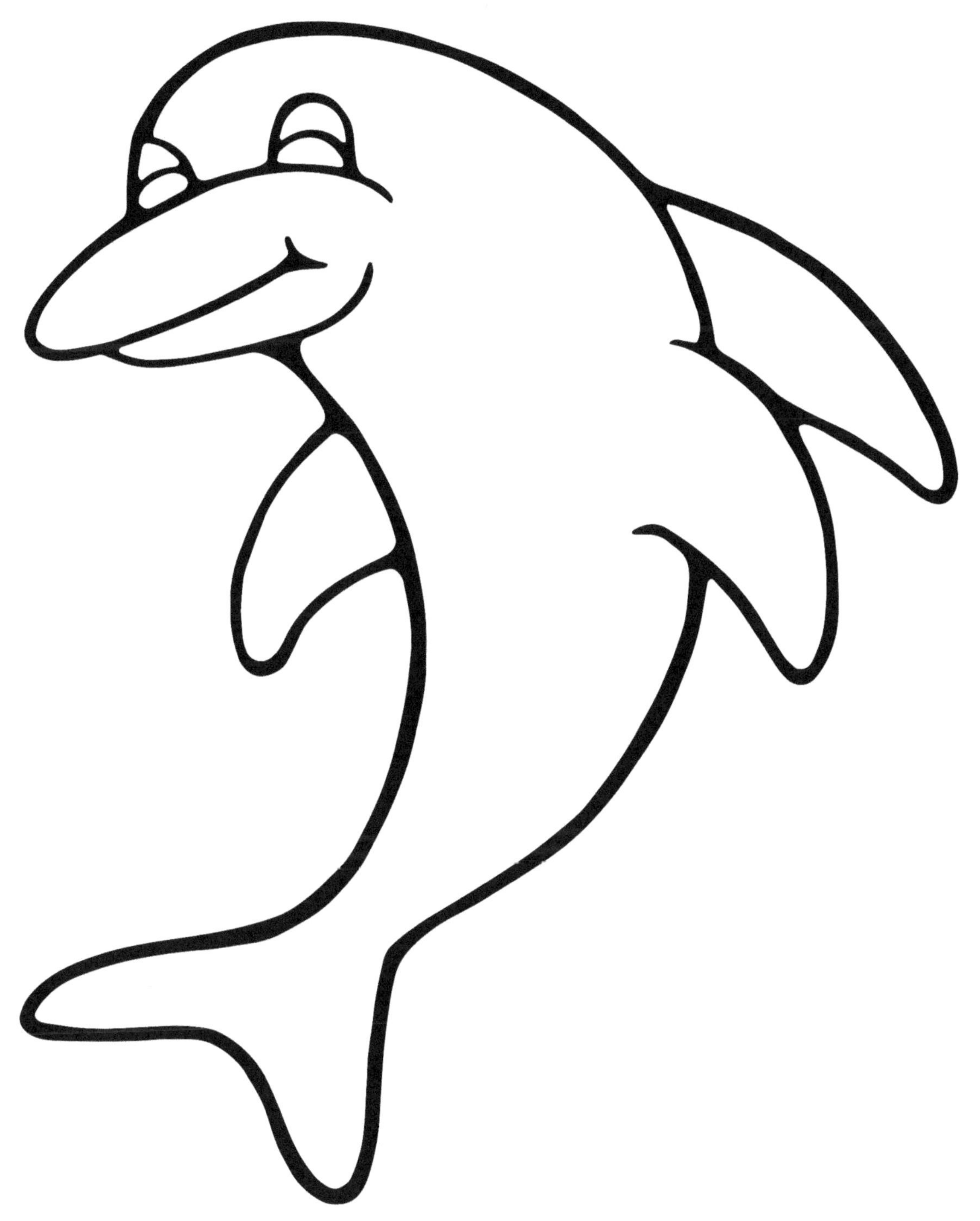

_____________ With The Dolphin's

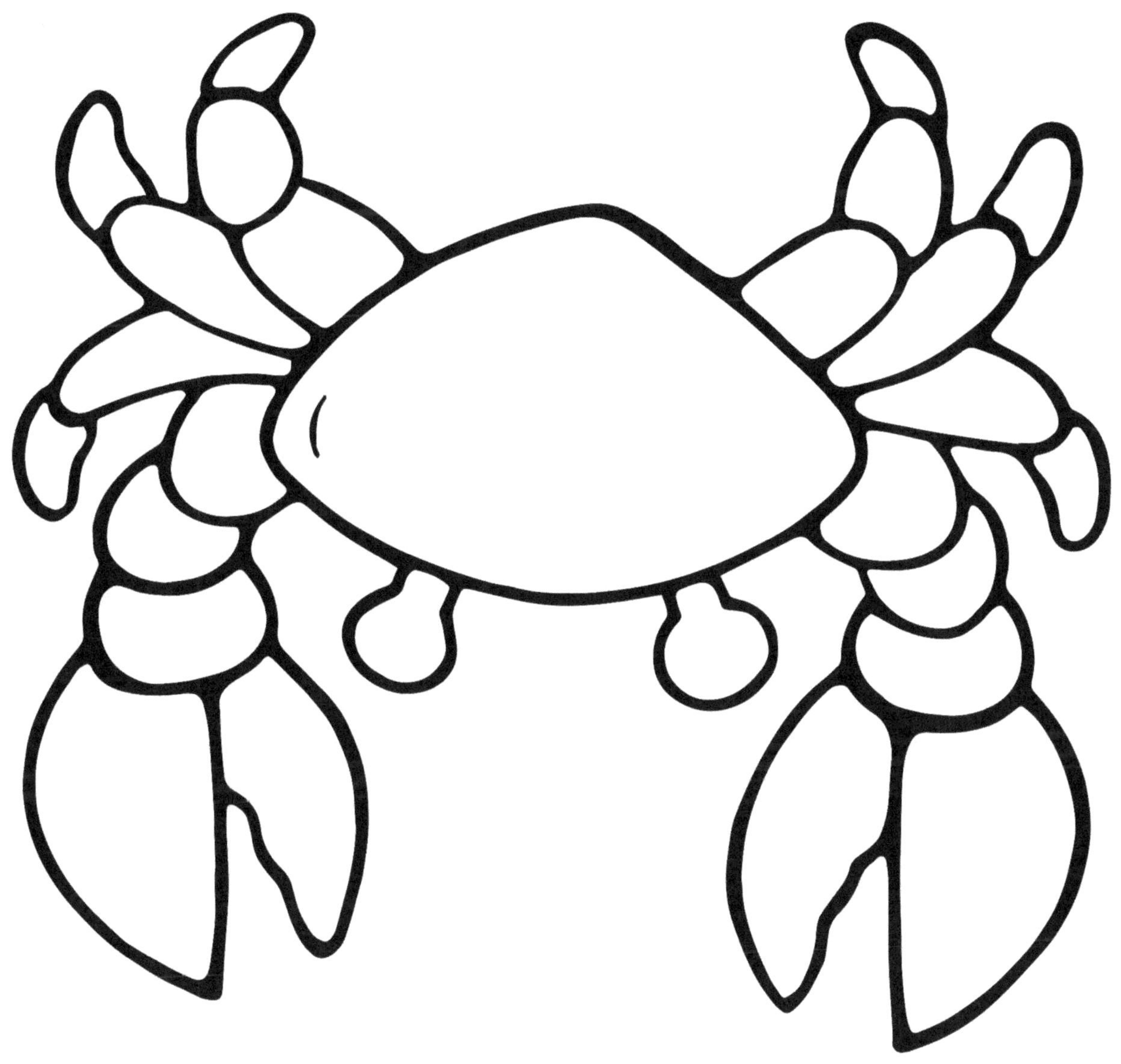

Crab ____________

Finding ________ Shells On The Beach

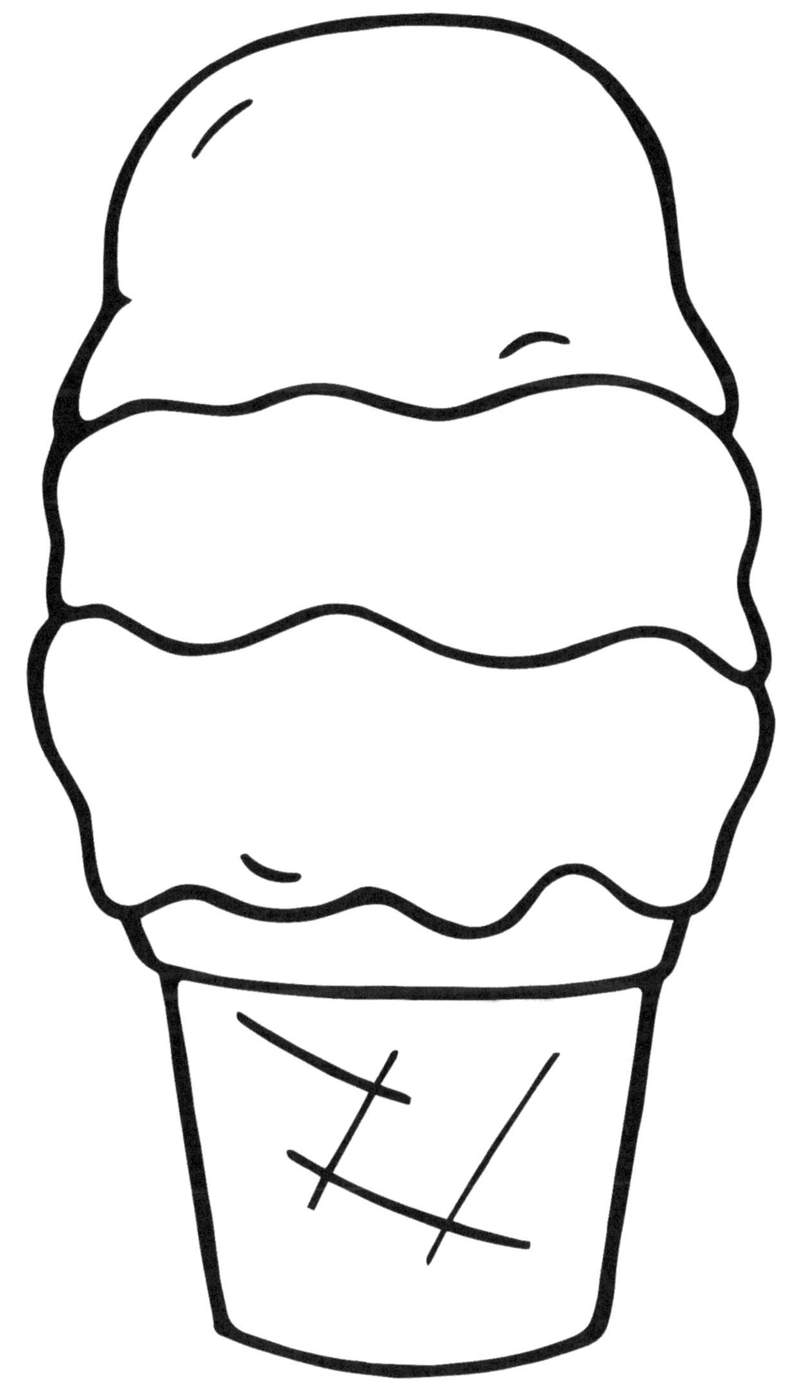

3 __________ Of Icecream

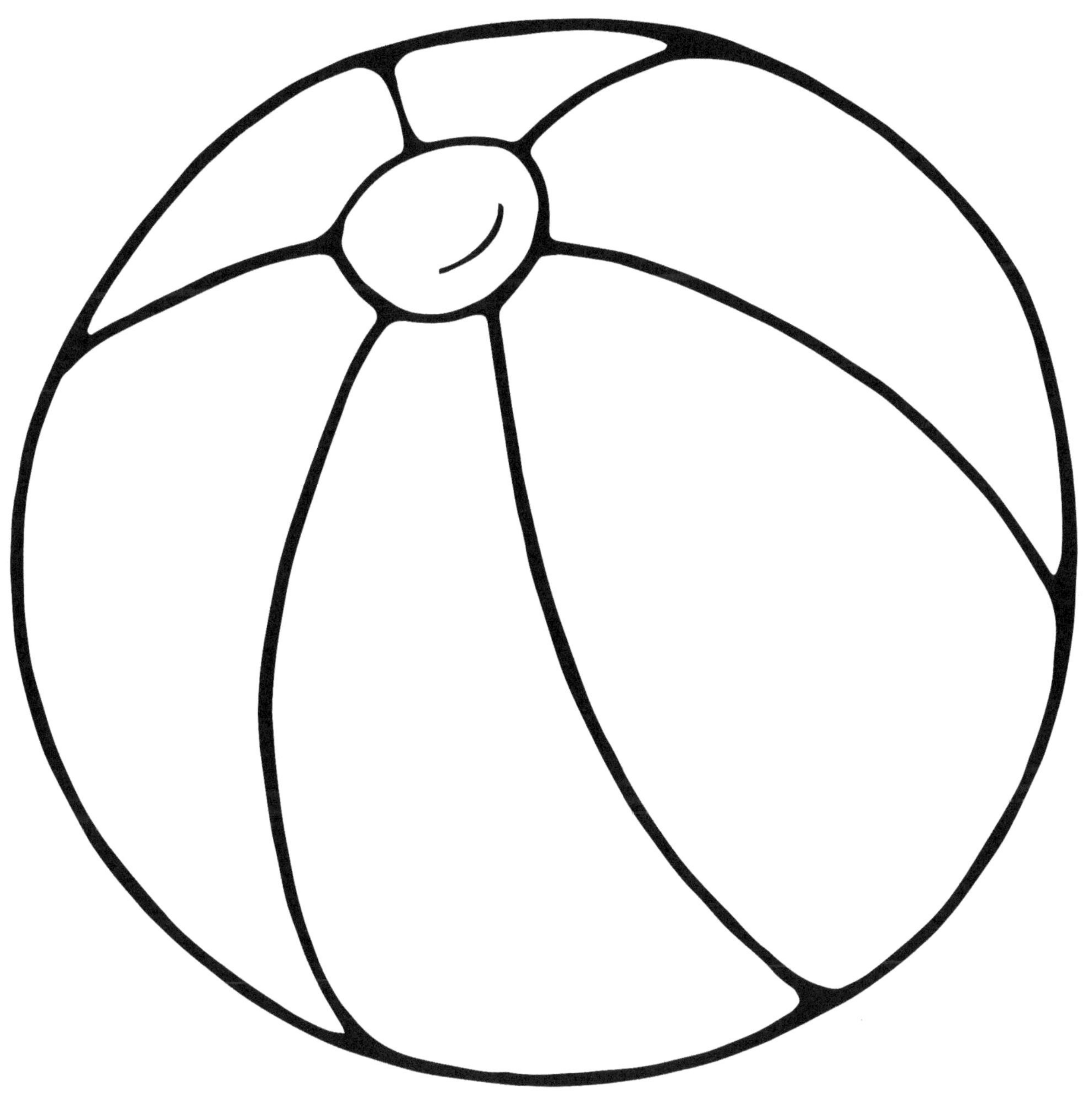

Summer ___________ Ball

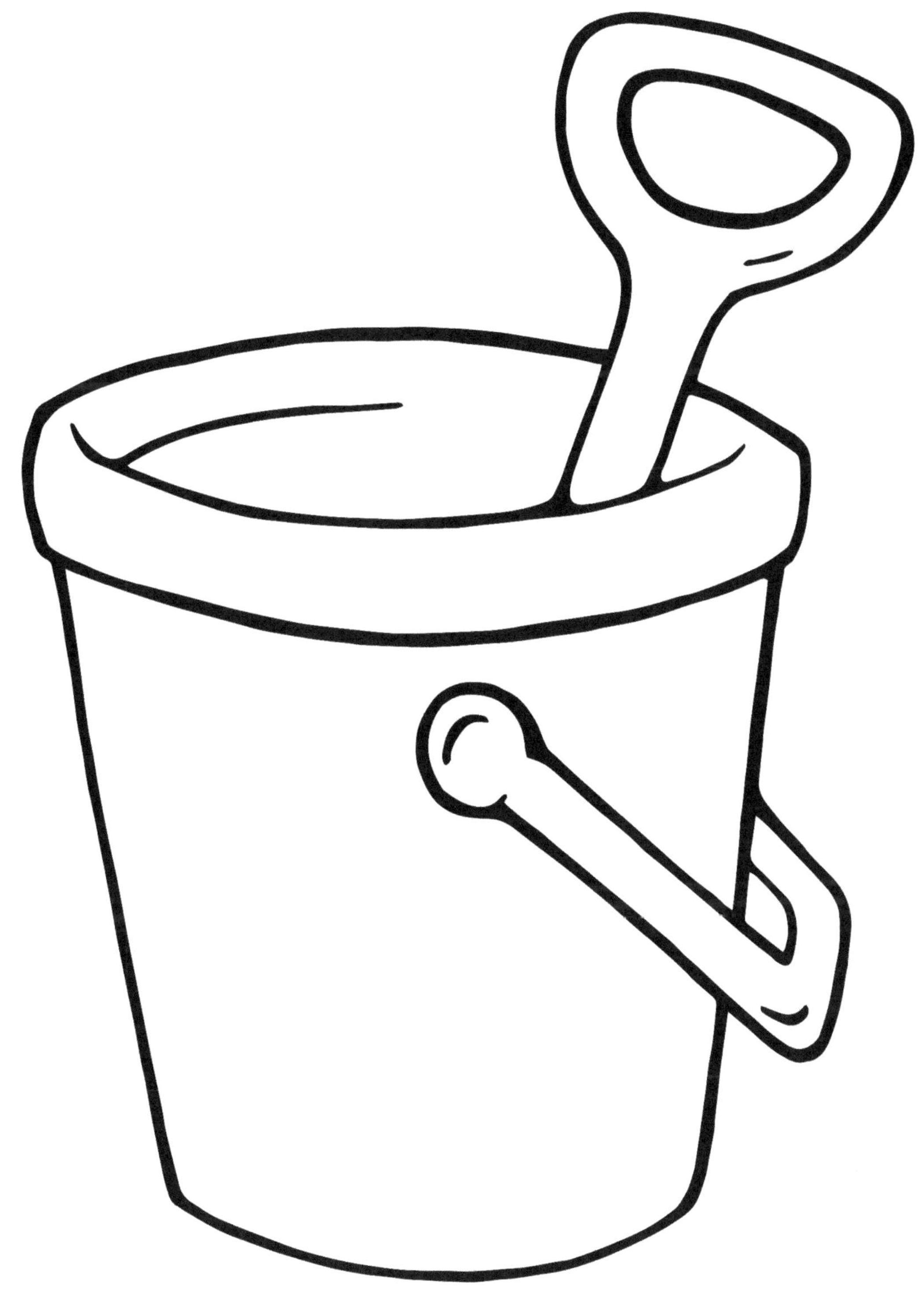

Sand Pail And ___________

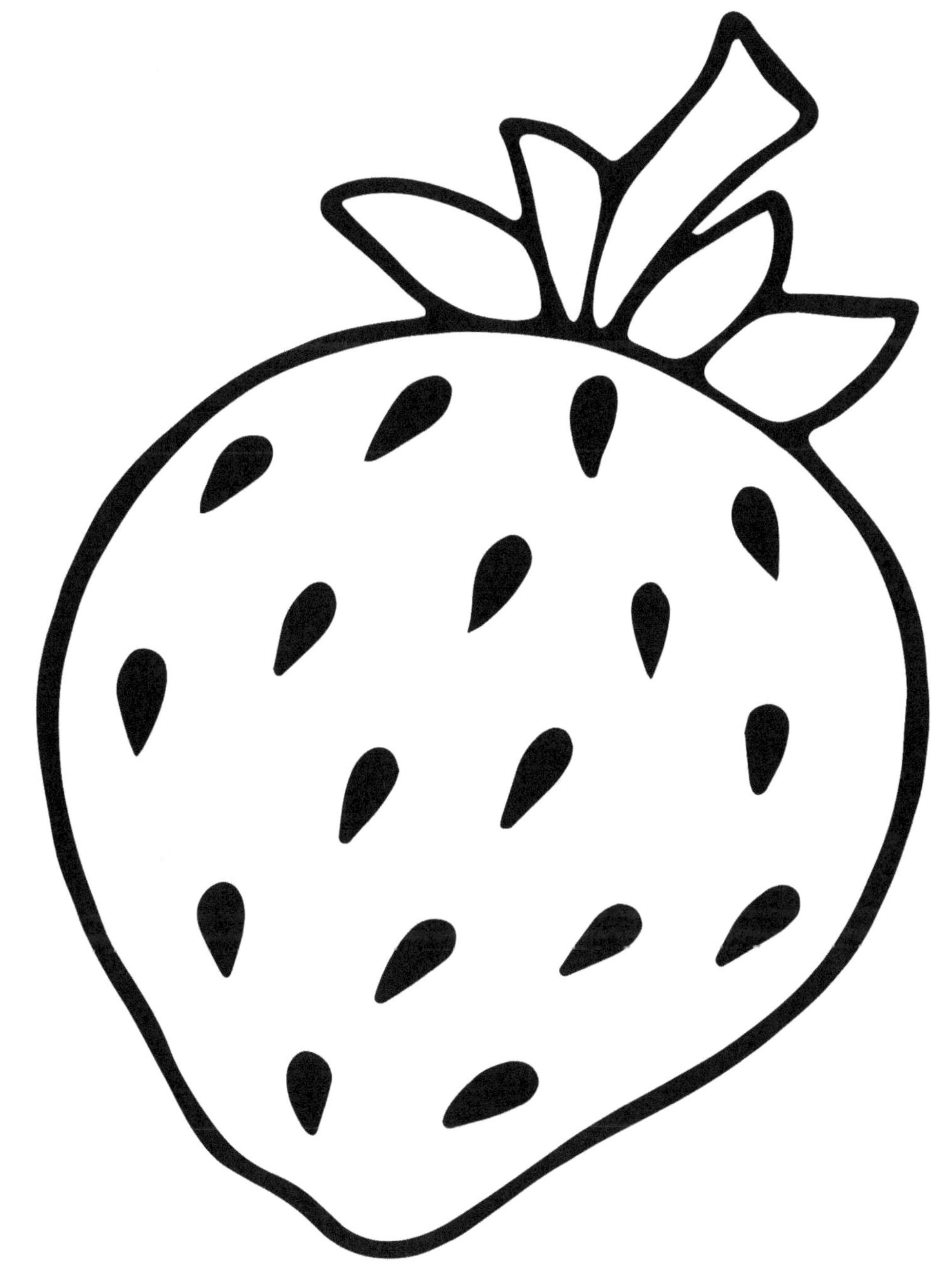

Strawberries And ___________

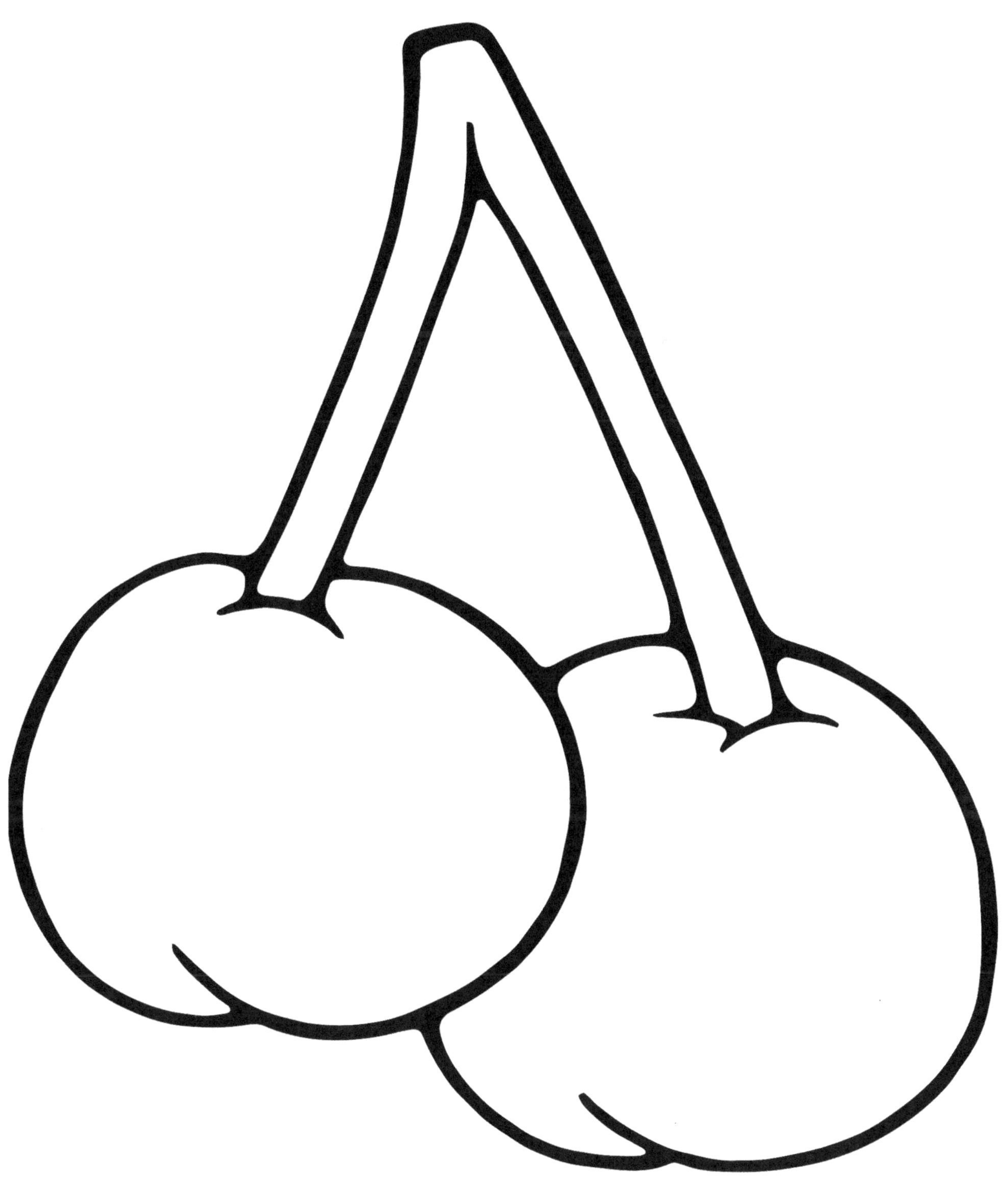

Cherry ___________

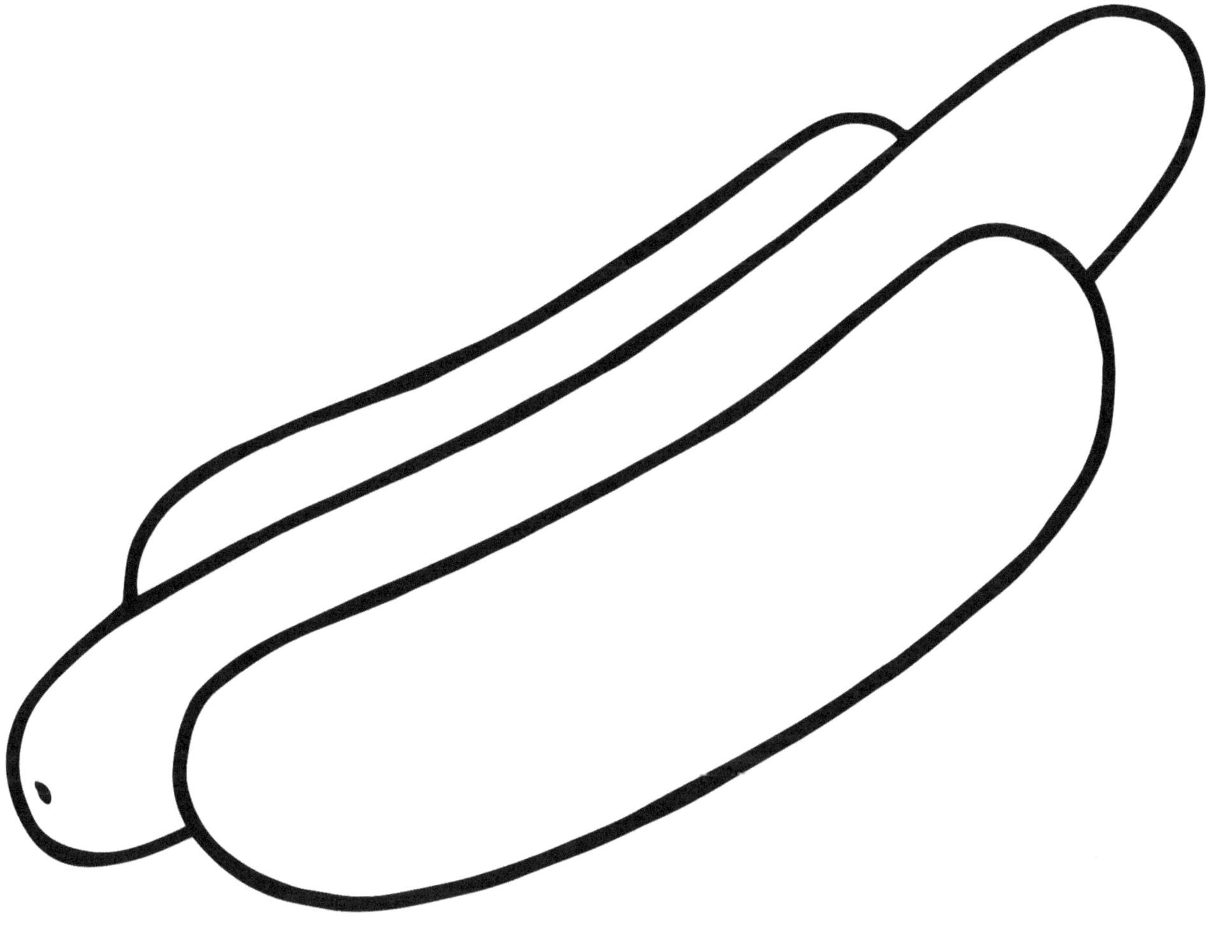

Hotdog On A Bun With ___________

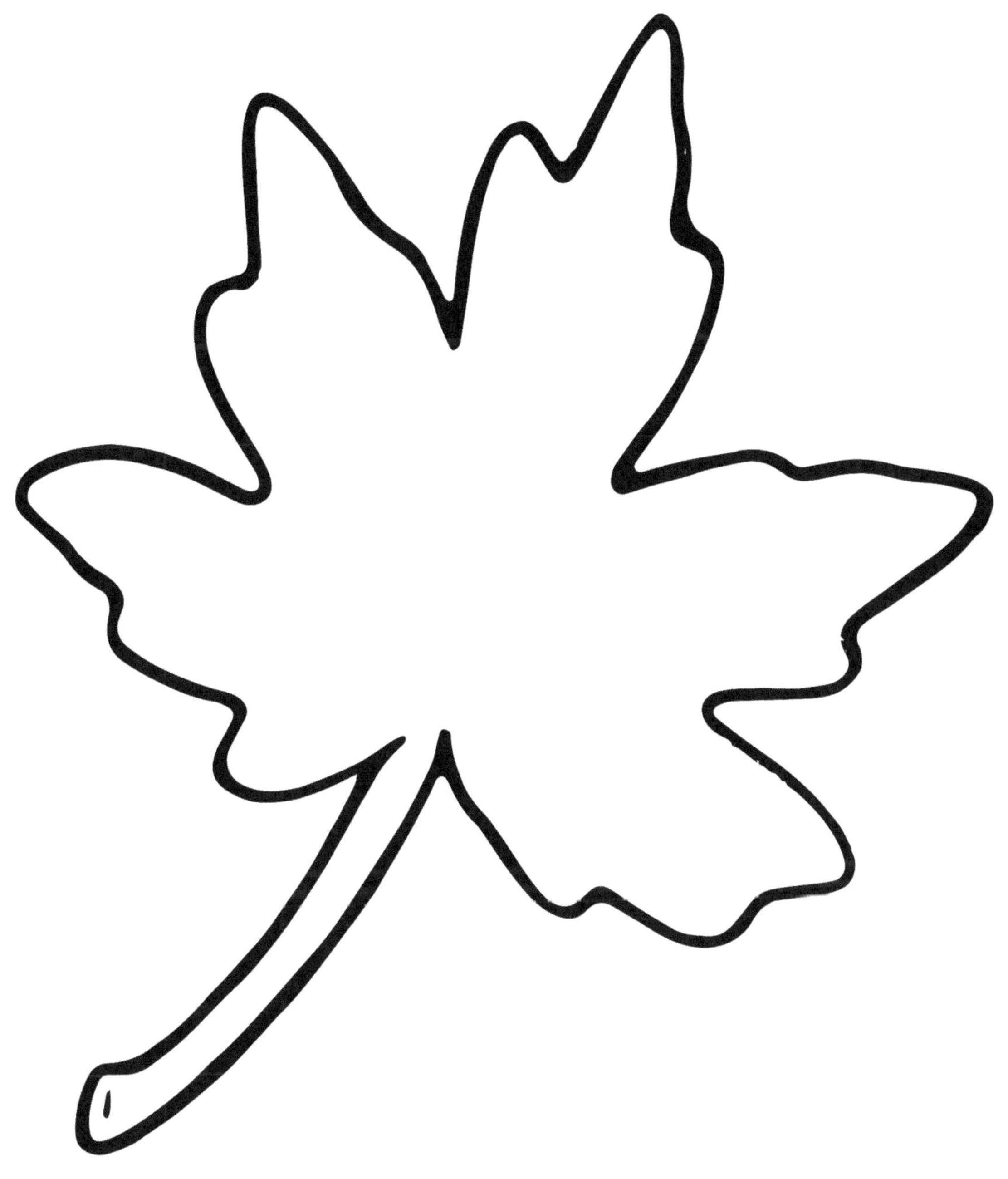

__________ Autumn Leaves

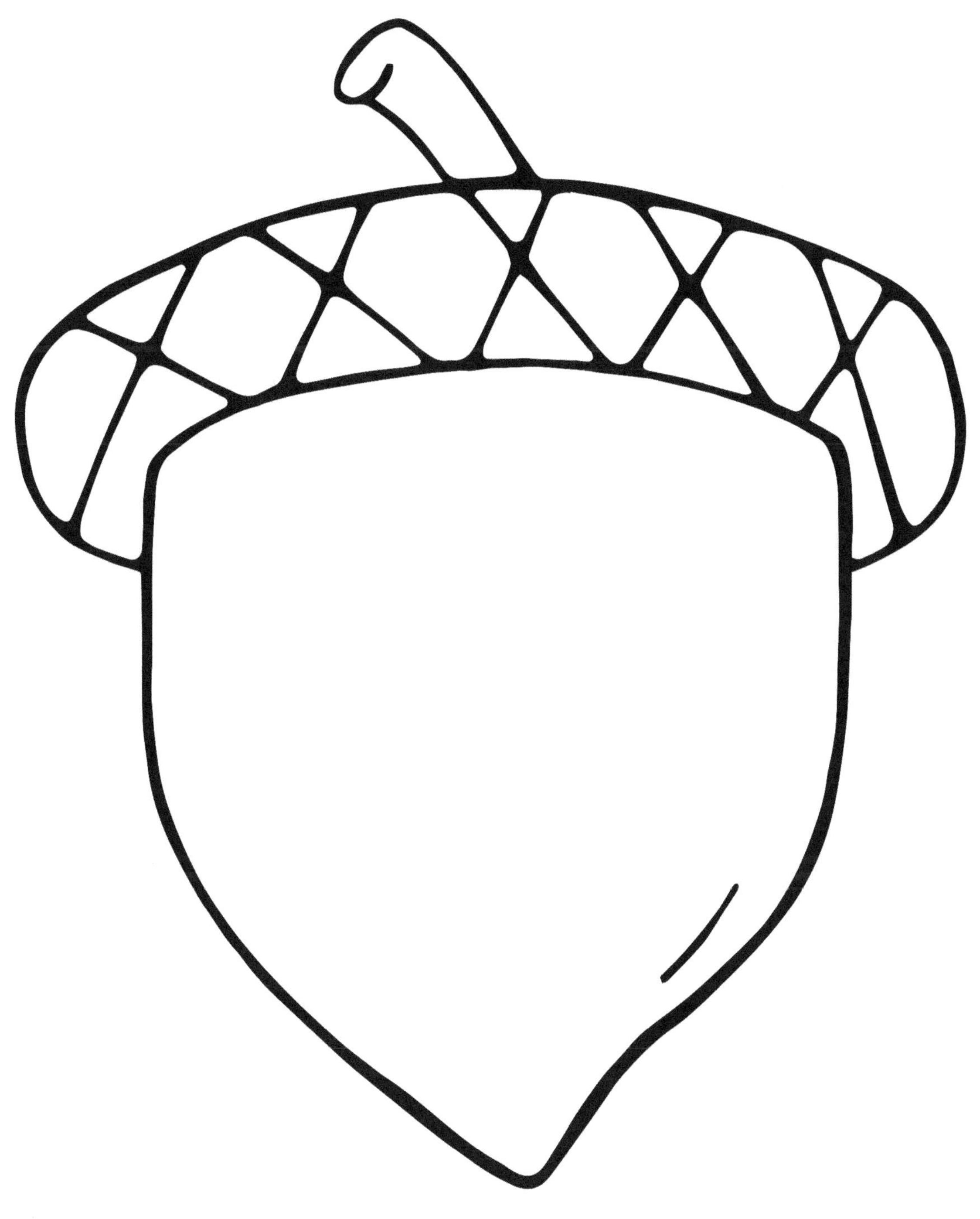

__________ Eat Acorns

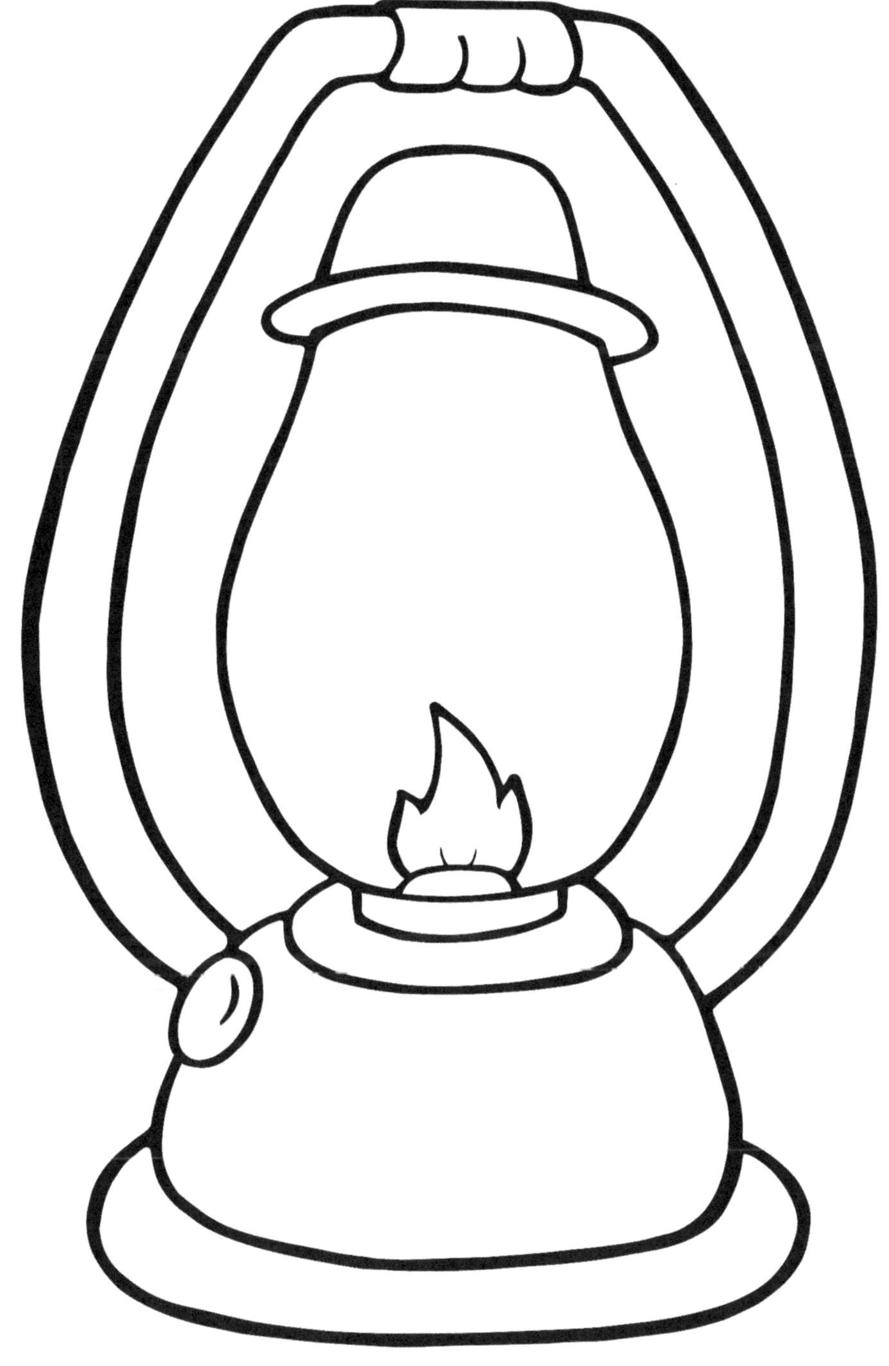

Keep The Lantern ___________

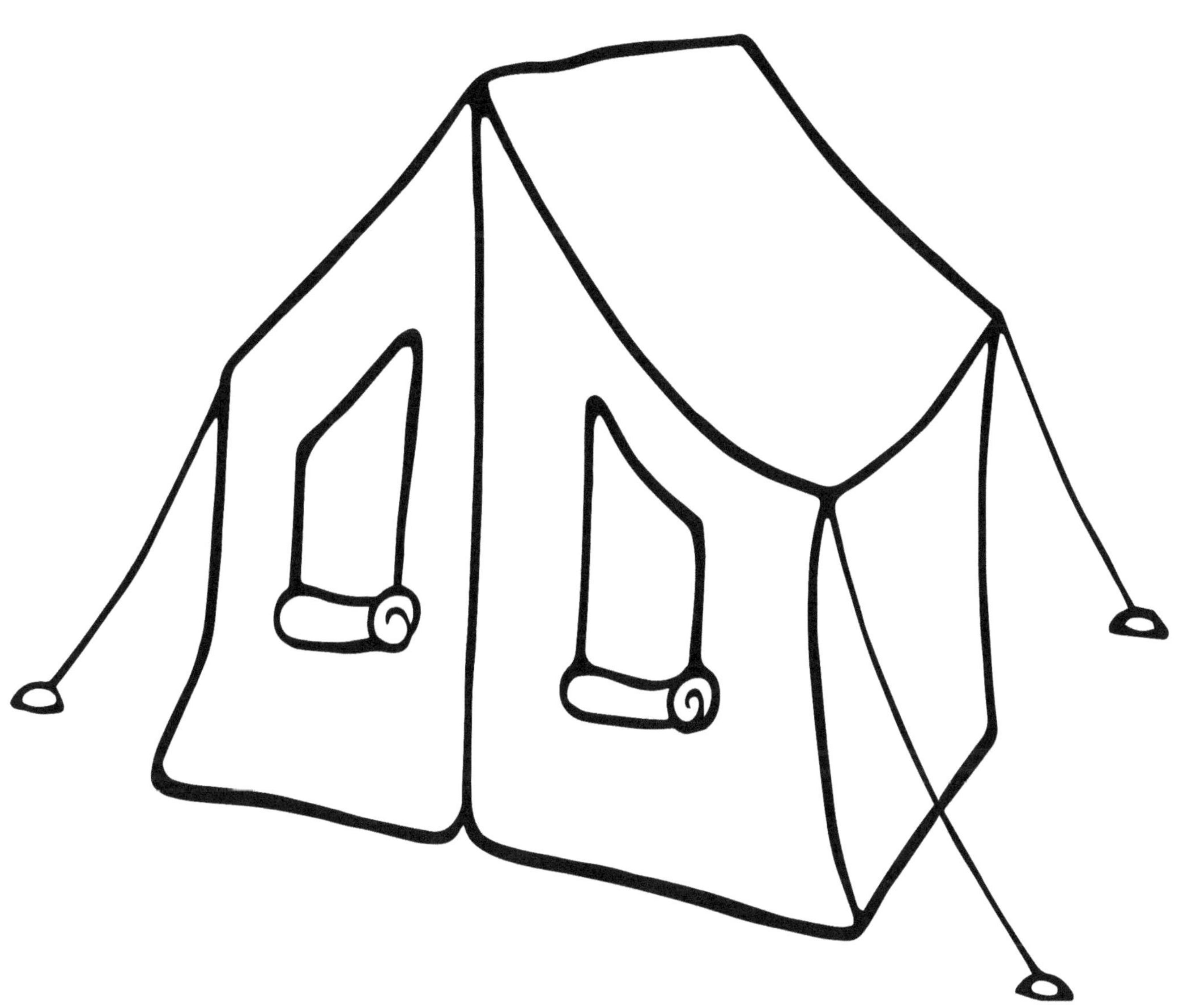

Pitch A Tent In __________

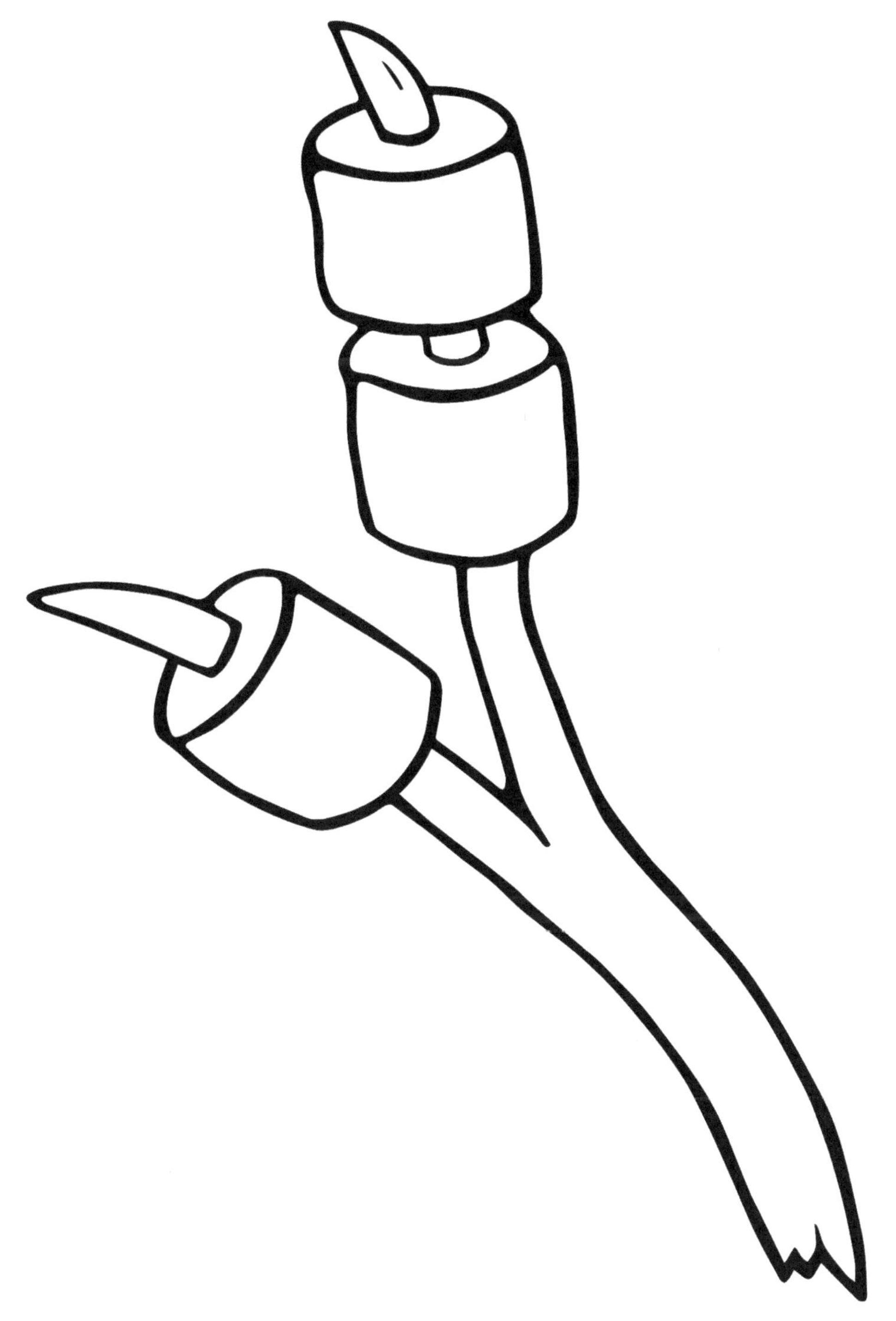

Marshmallows On A __________

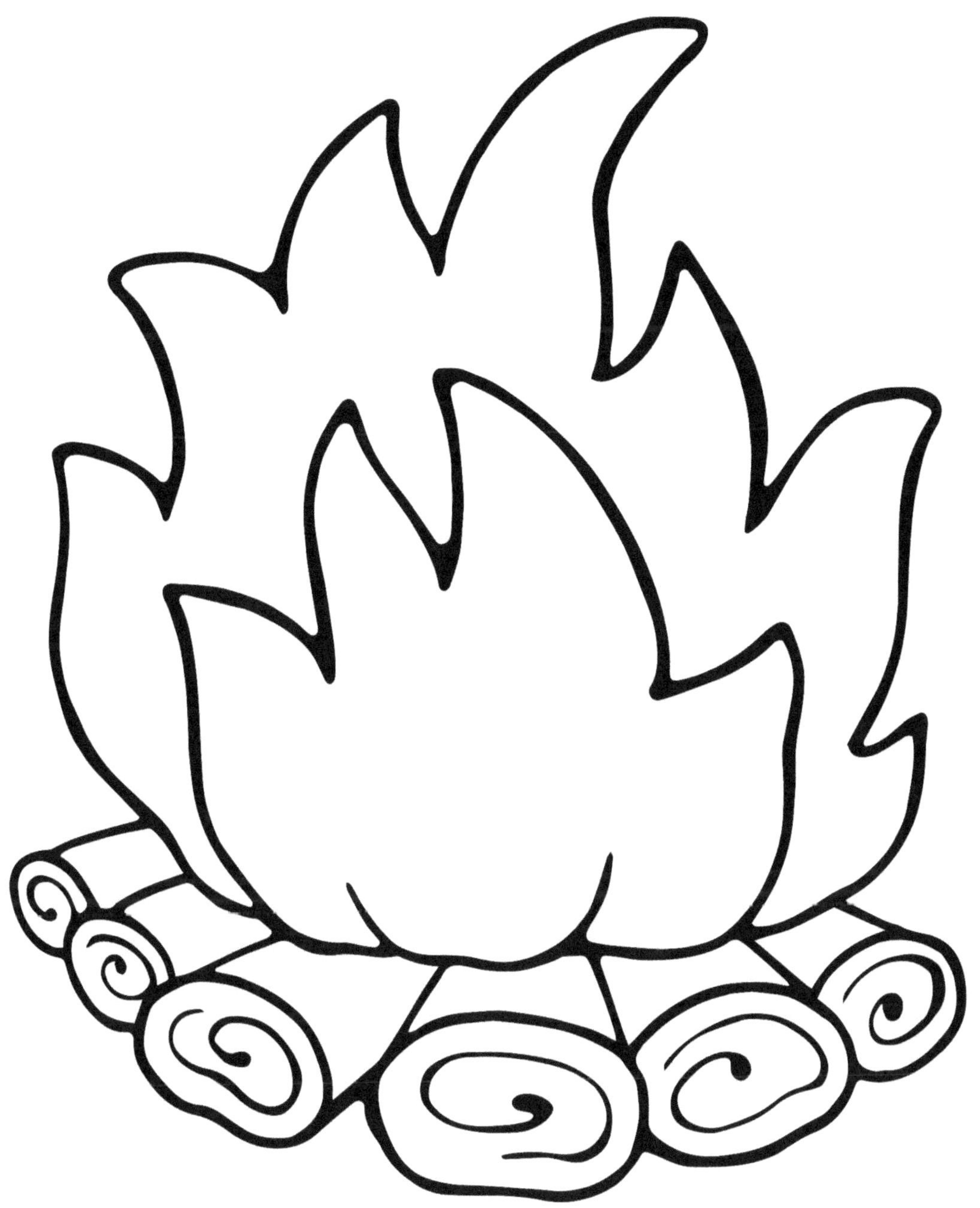

Summer ___________ Fire

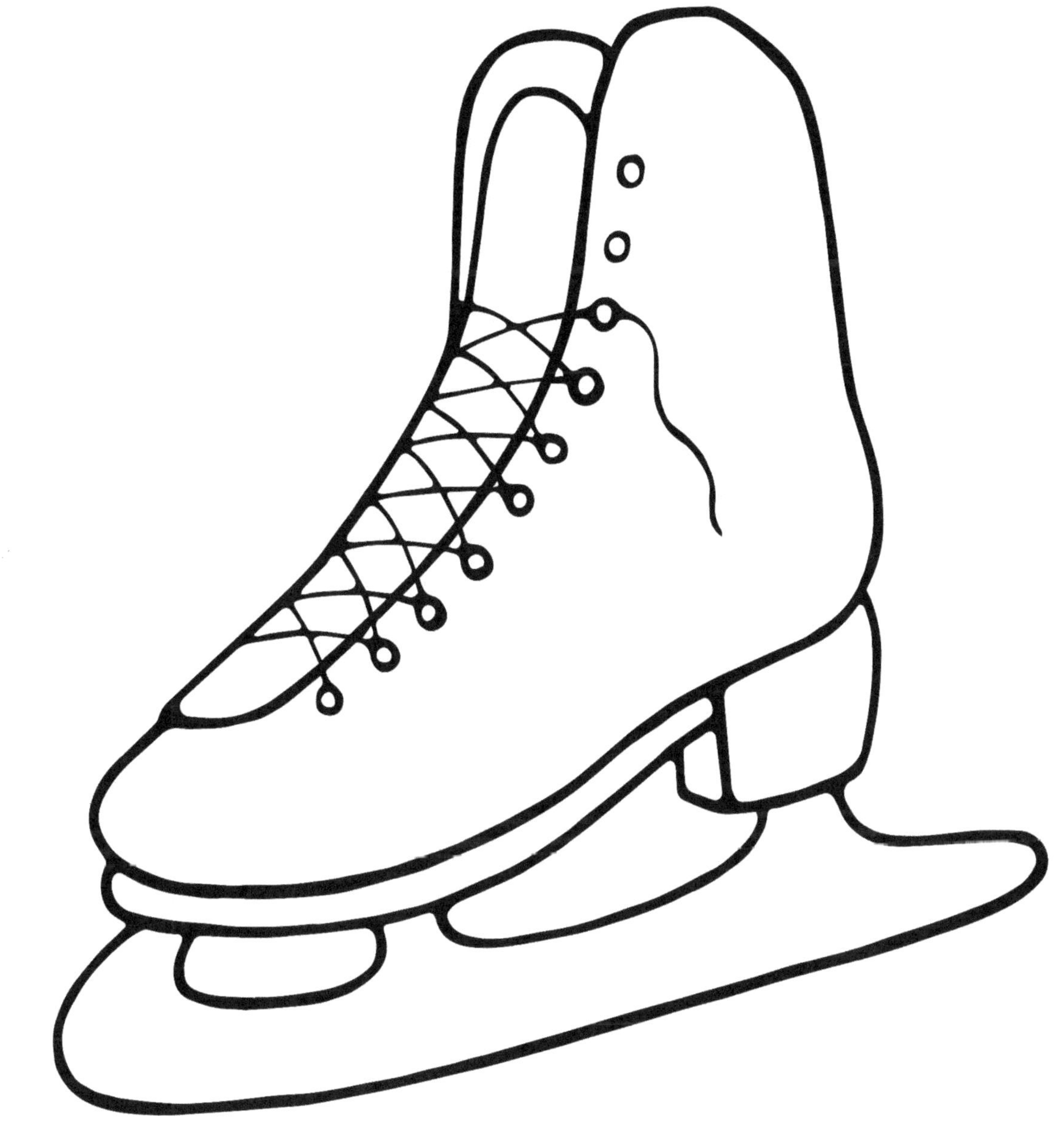

__________ Skating

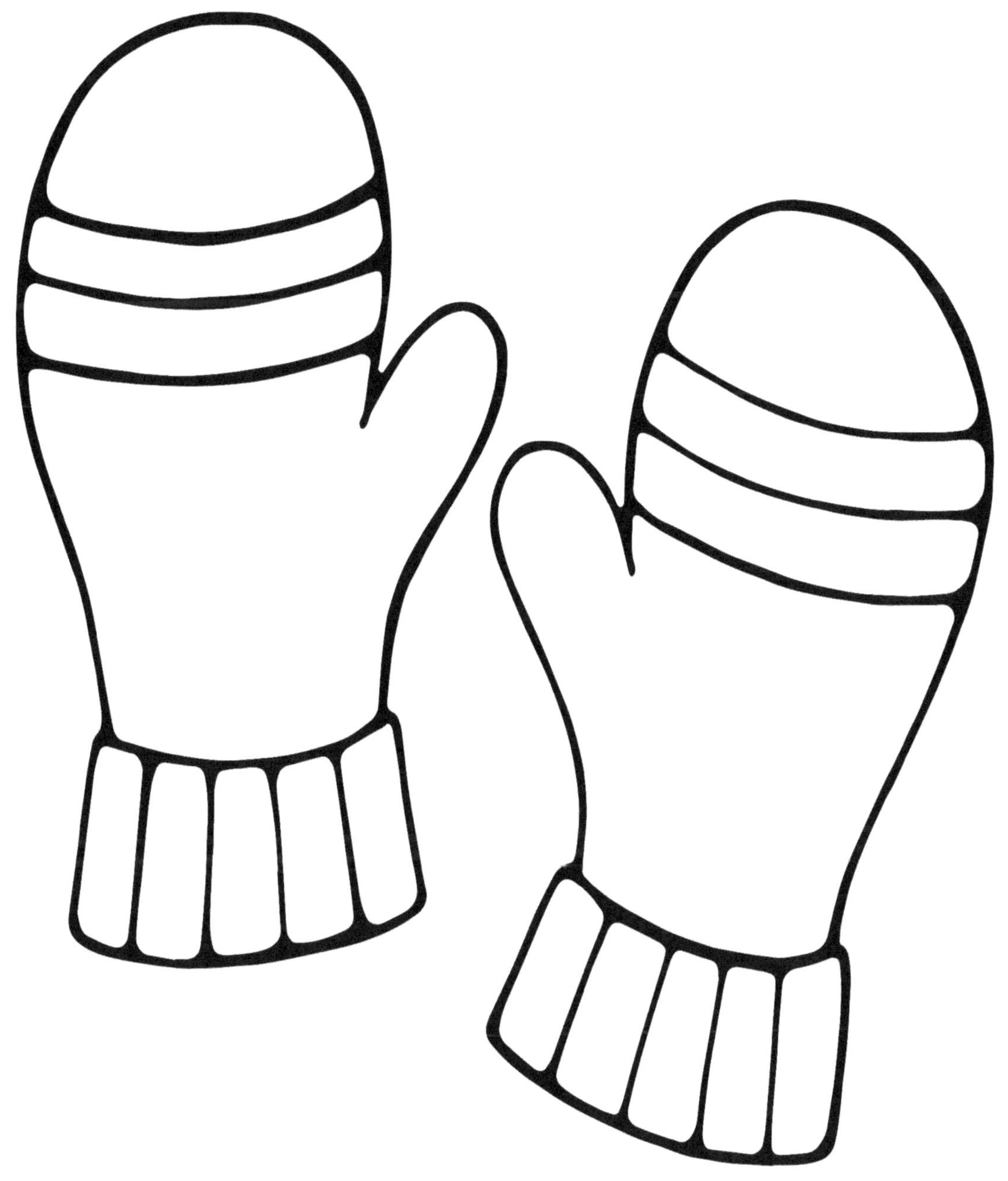

Knitted __________ Mittens

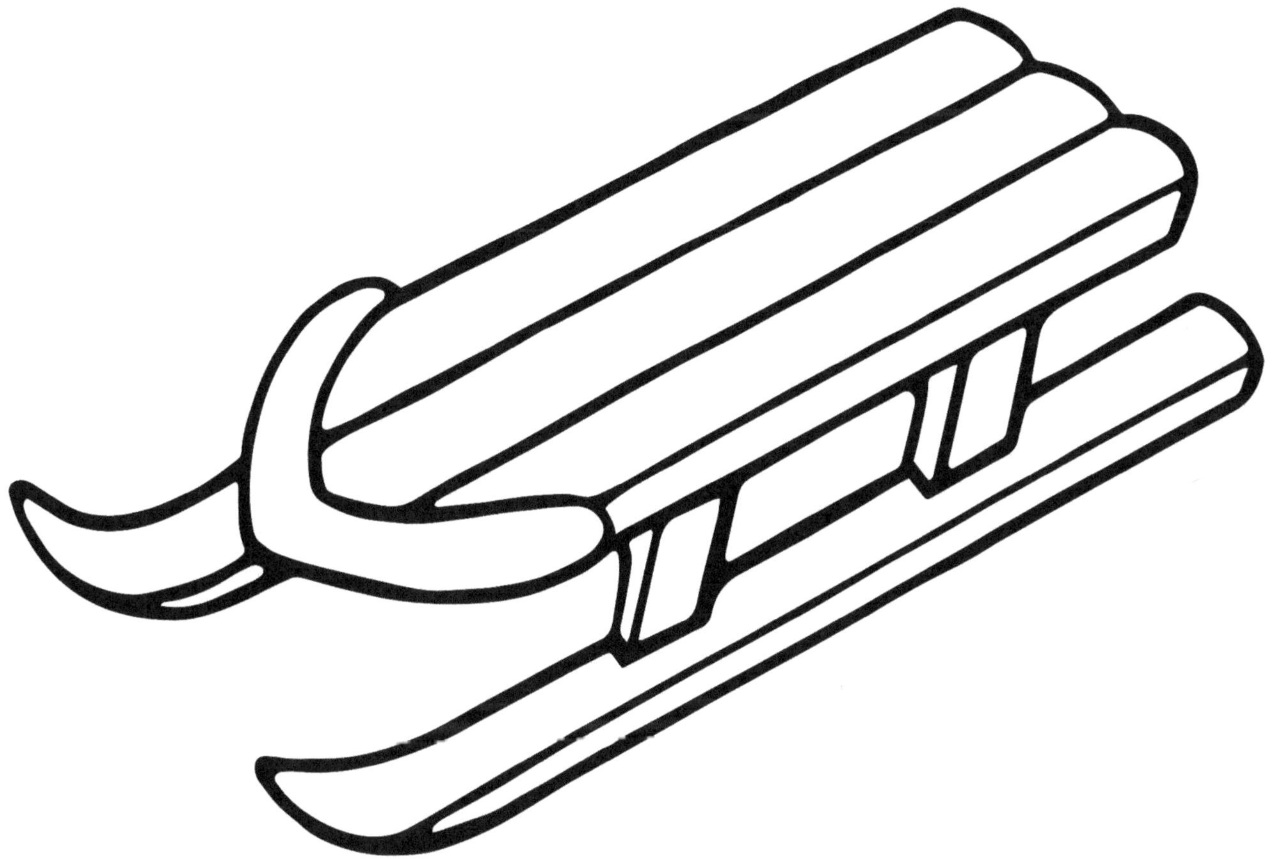

Sledding On __________

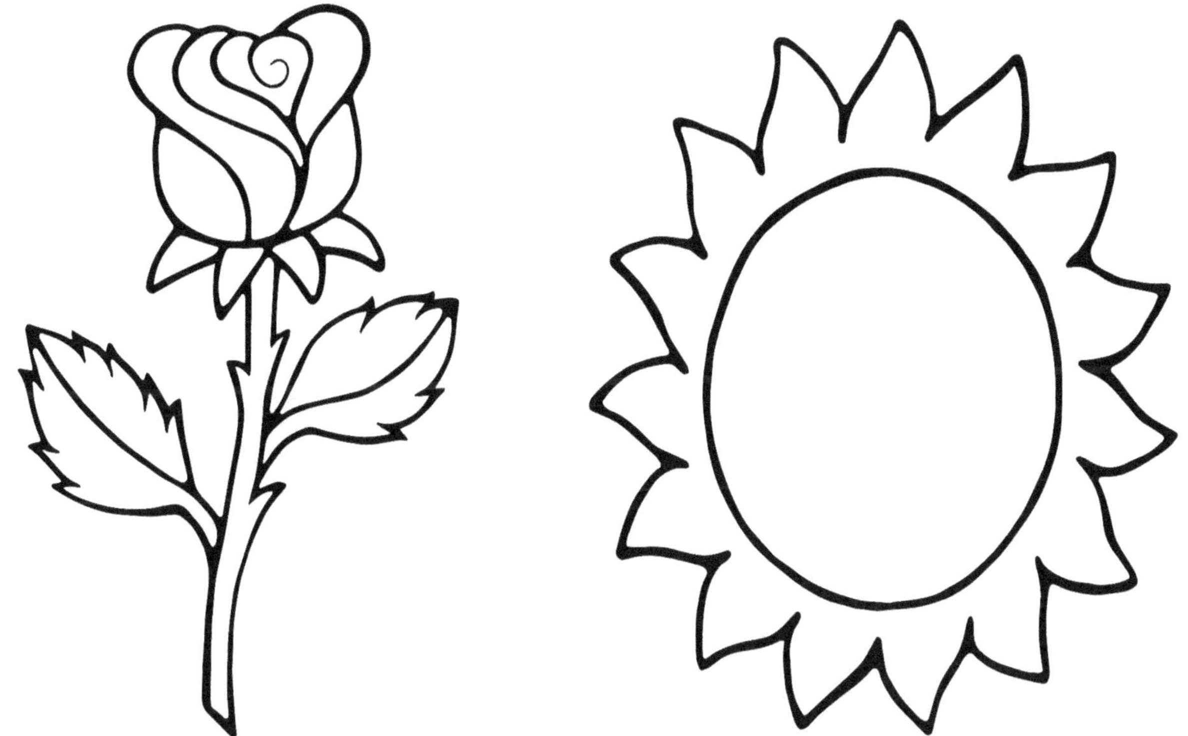

Journal - The 4-Seasons

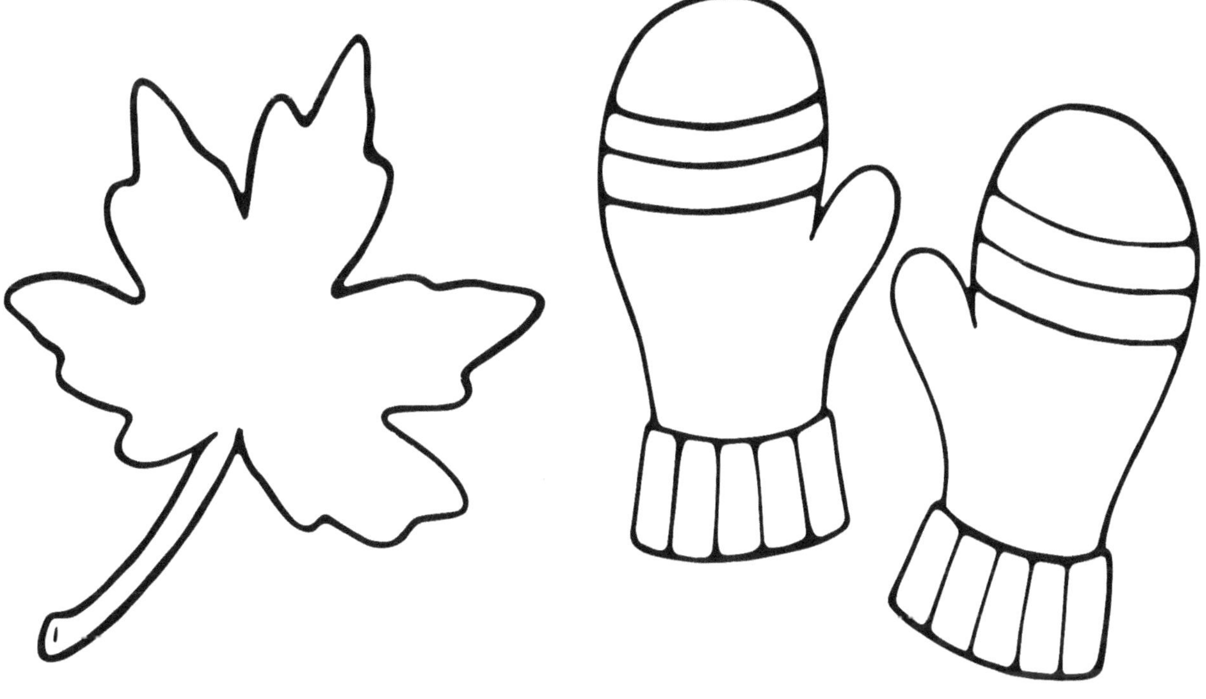

Spring - Memories

1

2

3

4

5

6

7

8

9

10

11

Spring - Memories

1

2

3

4

5

6

7

8

9

10

11

Remembering The 4-Seasons - ArtZillustrations.com

Summer - Memories

1

2

3

4

5

6

7

8

9

10

11

Summer - Memories

1

2

3

4

5

6

7

8

9

10

11

Remembering The 4-Seasons - ArtZillustrations.com

Autumn - Memories

1

2

3

4

5

6

7

8

9

10

11

Autumn - Memories

1

2

3

4

5

6

7

8

9

10

11

Remembering The 4-Seasons - ArtZillustrations.com

Winter - Memories

1

2

3

4

5

6

7

8

9

10

11

Remembering The 4-Seasons - ArtZillustrations.com

Winter - Memories

1

2

3

4

5

6

7

8

9

10

11

Remembering The 4-Seasons - ArtZillustrations.com

Go To ArtZillustrations.com For More
Interactive Coloring Books, Adult Coloring Books, Journals & Products

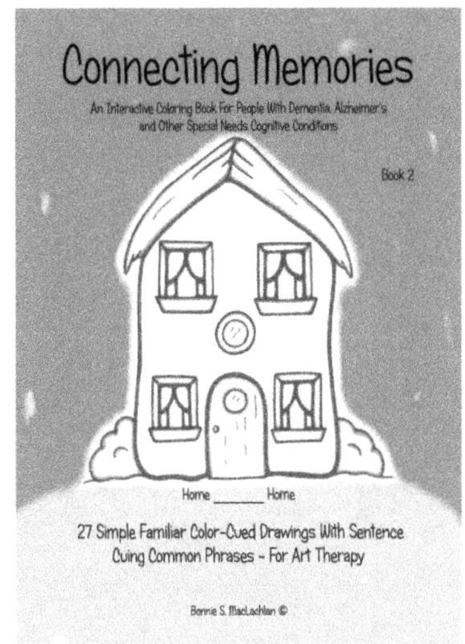

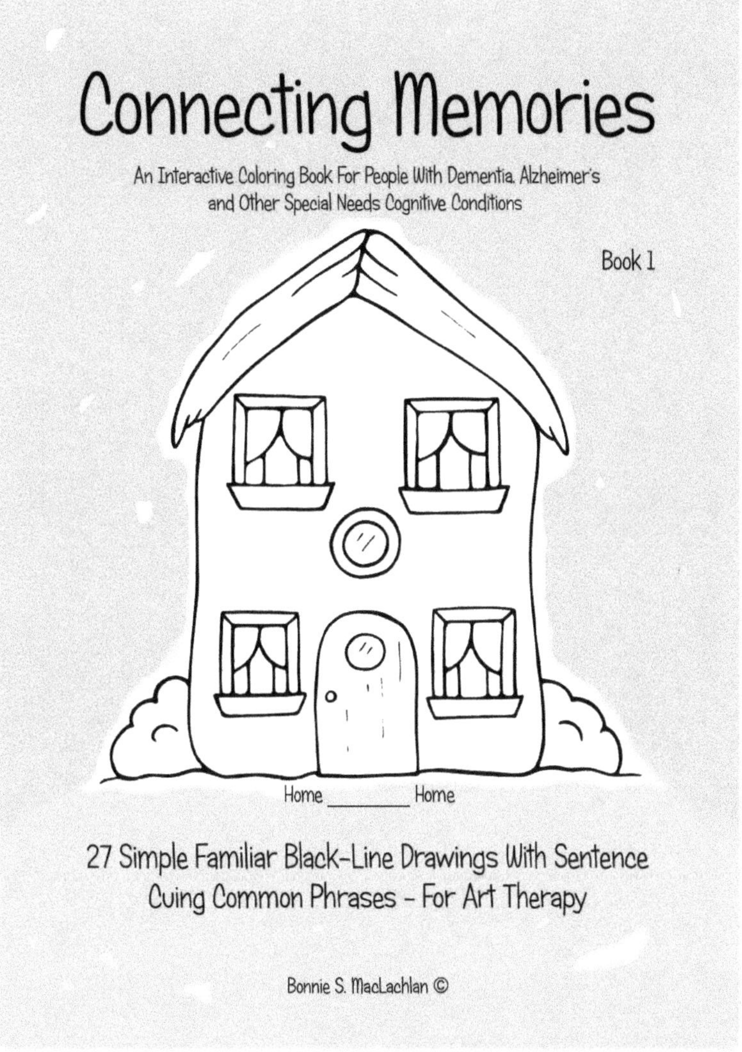

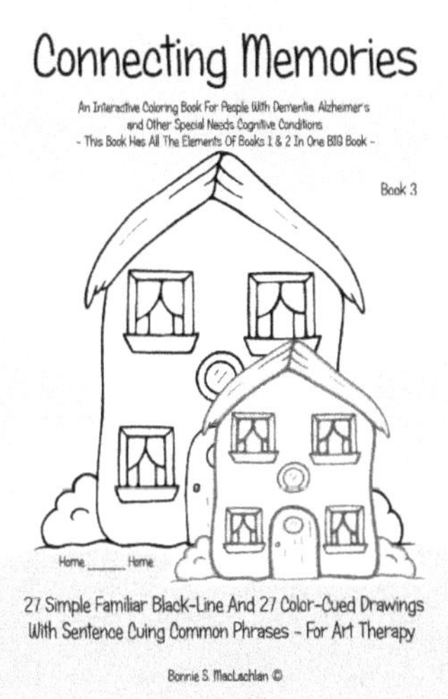

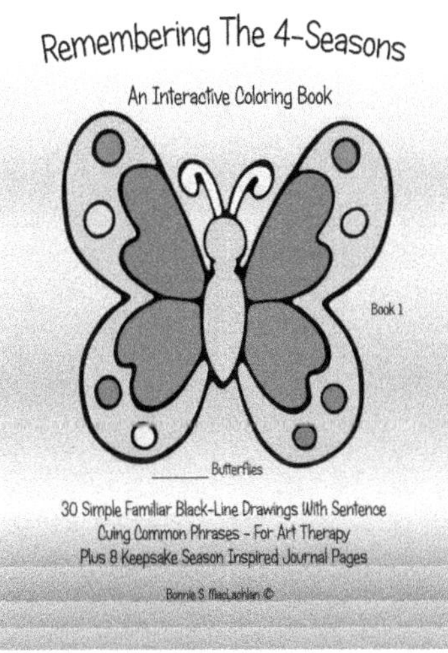

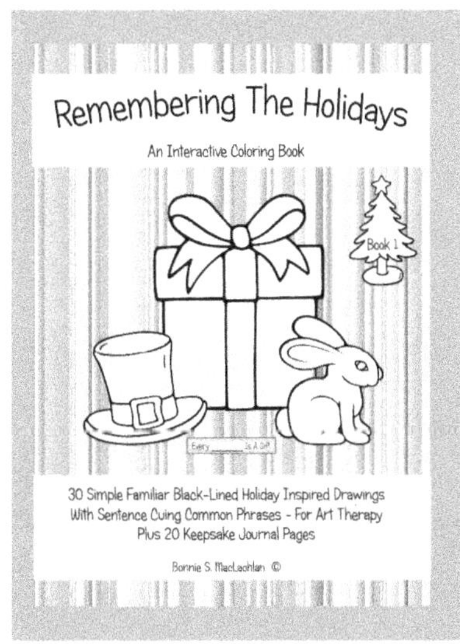

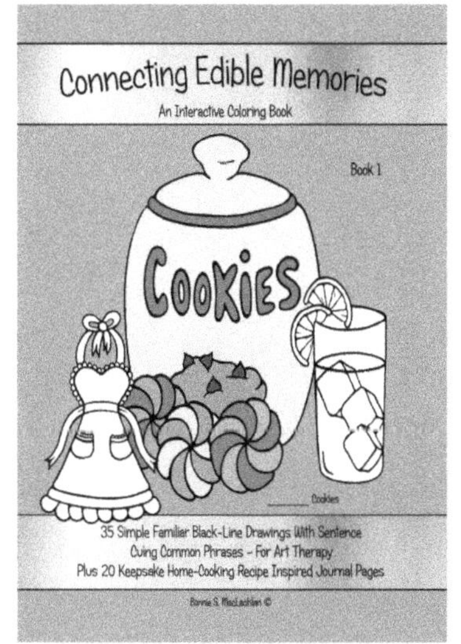

www.ingramcontent.com/pod-product-compliance
Lightning Source LLC
LaVergne TN
LVHW081421110826
845149LV00010B/1819

* 9 7 8 0 9 9 7 7 8 8 9 0 7 *